MW01517711

HUMOR

EMOTIONAL ASPECTS, ROLE IN SOCIAL INTERACTIONS AND HEALTH EFFECTS

PSYCHOLOGY OF EMOTIONS, MOTIVATIONS AND ACTIONS

Additional books in this series can be found on Nova's website under the Series tab.

Additional e-books in this series can be found on Nova's website under the eBooks tab.

PSYCHOLOGY OF EMOTIONS, MOTIVATIONS AND ACTIONS

HUMOR

EMOTIONAL ASPECTS, ROLE IN SOCIAL INTERACTIONS AND HEALTH EFFECTS

HOLLY PHILLIPS

EDITOR

nova
publishers
New York

Library of Congress Cataloging-in-Publication Data

Names: Phillips, Holly, 1979- editor.
Title: Humor: emotional aspects, role in social interactions and health
    effects / editor, Holly Phillips.
Other titles: Humor (Nova Science Publishers)
Description: Hauppauge, New York: Nova Science Publishers, Inc., [2016] |
    Series: Psychology of emotions, motivations and actions | Includes index.
Identifiers: LCCN 2016004829 (print) | LCCN 2016013138 (ebook) | ISBN
    9781634847872 (hardcover) | ISBN 9781634848022 ()
Subjects: LCSH: Laughter--Psychological aspects. | Wit and
    humor--Psychological aspects. | Wit and humor--Therapeutic use.
Classification: LCC BF575.L3 H8735 2016 (print) | LCC BF575.L3 (ebook) | DDC
    152.4/3--dc23
LC record available at http://lccn.loc.gov/2016004829

Published by Nova Science Publishers, Inc. † New York

CONTENTS

PREFACE

Expression of humor begins at an early age in humans and it arises from both cognitive and social-emotional developmental origins. This book presents research on the emotional aspects, role in social interaction, and the health effects of humor. Chapter One begins with a discussion on social-emotional and cognitive aspects of humor, and suggests that the interactions among these developmental factors provide impetus for the expression and appreciation of humor, even during early childhood. Chapter Two supports the Theory of the Absurd and the Empowerment theory as a framework of unfolding the clowning behaviors of a kindergartener and provides a positive way of considering clowning during the early childhood years highlighting its importance to play and social empowerment. Chapter Three studies the impact of humor of closeness to neighbors. Chapter Four aims to bridge the gap between theory and practice in the fields of social cognition, identity, and humor within adolescence. Chapter Five explores some of the ways that humor may influence workplace health and well-being, while also addressing some of the problematic aspects of humor use. Chapter Six explores areas of healthcare where the deployment of humor or response to patient-initiated humor and/or laughter by a health profession would be considered inappropriate by their peers and/or their patient and/or the patients' family and friends. Chapter Seven analyzes instances of a specific kind of humor that has been identified as jocular mockery because of its frequent occurrence in intimate and close relationships among friends.

In: Humor   ISBN: 978-1-63484-787-2
Editor: Holly Phillips   © 2016 Nova Science Publishers, Inc.

Chapter 1

HUMOR DEVELOPMENT: COGNITIVE, EMOTIONAL, AND SOCIAL INTERACTIONS

Doris Bergen·
Distinguished Professor Emerita,
Miami University, Oxford, OH, US

ABSTRACT

Expression of humor begins at an early age in humans and it arises from both cognitive and social-emotional developmental origins. These early origins and courses of development have been documented by many theorists and researchers (e.g., Freud, 1960; Klein, 2003; McGhee, 1979; Pien & Rothbart, 1976; Schwekbe & Gryski, 2003; Wolfenstein, 1978). Some of them have emphasized the social-emotional aspects (e.g., Freud, Schwekbe & Gryski, Wolfenstein) while others have focused on cognitive aspects (e.g., Klein, McGhee, Pien & Rothbart). This chapter discusses both of these perspectives and suggests that the interactions among these developmental factors provide the impetus for the expression and appreciation of humor, even during early childhood. Studies of humor development over the age period from infancy to elementary age by the author and others are discussed, and recent research on the humor of gifted elementary age students (Bergen, 2015) is reported that supports this interactive perspective. The discussion also

· Email: bergend@miamioh.edu.

addresses the role of humor as a facilitator of cognitive, emotional, and social interactions.

INTRODUCTION

Humor expression and appreciation are pervasive characteristics of the human species and they become evident even in the first year of a child's life. The ability both to appreciate and to generate humor can continue to develop throughout life and to influence many other areas of development. As with most human characteristics, however, this ability is more highly developed in some individuals than in others, and the environment in which children are raised can affect their humor development as well as their cognitive, emotional, and social skills. There are a number of reasons why this variation in humor expression and appreciation might occur, including genetic predispositions, family environments, humor models, and success in using humor to enhance cognitive, emotional, and social development.

The ways that humor may facilitate cognitive, social, and emotional qualities have been of interest to researchers and theorists from many professional fields. However, the focus of much of this study has been on the ways various types of humor expression are related to adult cognitive and social-emotional interactions, rather than to how humor development may be an influence on children's cognitive, social, and emotional development. There has been a growing body of research on childhood humor development in recent years, especially focused on how it may facilitate or accompany to other developmental areas in childhood and theorists and researchers from a number of theoretical perspectives have discussed this interface and observed changes in humor behaviors over the childhood years. There have been two main areas of theoretical and research interest. One is regarding the interface between humor and cognitive development and the other is between humor and social-emotional development. There also has been some study of how humor develops in special populations of children; for example, children who are cognitively gifted or those who have social-emotional communication issues such as autism. More recently, there has been study of how positive and negative aspects of children's humor expression may be related to children's social acceptance by other children (e.g., use in social media or bullying in school). As is the case with every area of human development, there are strategies that adults can use to foster and strengthen children's humor development and make it a force that supports both cognitive and social-emotional growth.

THEORETICAL PERSPECTIVES ON CHILDREN'S HUMOR DEVELOPMENT

The two major strands of theoretical and research interest have been focused on ways that humor development may parallel, demonstrate, and enhance cognitive development and social-emotional development.

Humor and Cognitive Development. The cognitive aspects of humor development, in particular those related to humor that is based on resolution of incongruity, have been of interest to a number of theorists and researchers. Observers of young children have long noted that much early childhood humor demonstrates the children's growing understanding of what "should be." In supportive and benign environments, infant laughter often gives clues to what the child has already learned and toddlers are adept at doing something in a "wrong" way and laughing at their "joke." Much of both adult and child humor is based on cognitive reasoning, taking what is known and changing it in a way that makes it funny to the people who "know what it should be." Pien and Rothbart (1976) have stated that reacting to incongruity is not the same as reacting to novelty because a novel stimulus is unexpected but "an incongruous stimulus is *mis*expected." (p. 3). That is, while laughter is often elicited when an unexpected stimulus occurs (e.g., when a block structure falls), incongruous humor has an element of planned surprise, in which a certain expectation is changed deliberately in order to make the "audience" laugh. The cognitive growth that accompanies young children's humor attempts and responses can be observed and charted through a number of developmental stages related to incongruity humor.

One observer of child humor, Paul McGhee (2002), drew on Piagetian theory (1962) to define four stages of humor development based on children's ability to both recognize incongruity and to perform incongruous acts. McGhee suggested that at first infant laughter does not have a cognitive aspect (it is a basic human behavior) and often occurs particularly with attachment figures. For example, a baby game such as peek-a-boo has both the attachment basis and a surprise element. By the second year of life, however, children begin making their own incongruous jokes, indicating that they now "know" how things should be. For example, they will use objects incorrectly and look

for laughter (*incongruous actions*) or misname objects or play with words
(*incongruous language*). Although children recognize incongruous actions
with laughter (e.g., a picture of a dog wearing a hat) before they can generate
such actions, by age two most children will laugh at juxtaposed unrelated
objects and perform incongruous actions themselves. Recognitions of
incongruous acts or concepts often come through book reading activities with
parents. Young children's laughter at "incorrect" actions or words in pictures
or storybooks is a good indicator of their developing cognitive competence.

The second type of incongruity humor, *incongruous language*, which
begins about age 2, is often shown in sound play, such as chanting nonsense
words or repeating a song but changing the lyrics (Bergen, 1998). For
example, a child might substitute words in a song for other words, such as
singing "tuna butter" instead of "peanut butter" (in original song) and laughing
repeatedly at the substitution. This gradual development of the ability to
express incongruity in humorous actions and language begins with the ability
to differentiate between humorous actions or language and reality-based
actions or language. Thus, it provides strong evidence of cognitive growth.

Beginning about age 3 or 4, examples of *conceptual incongruity* can be
seen in children's humor behavior. Children will tell riddles and jokes that
have incongruity as the humor factor, and they begin to understand that
humorous behaviors are not incorrect but "rather of a pretend nature"
(Bariaud, 1989, p. 21). That is, for children to use various forms of humor,
they must distance themselves from the normative behaviors of reality. Young
children's ability to use "practical deception" in a playful way that generates
laughter is really an indication that they are aware that others may think
differently than they do and that they are "fooling" them (Sinclair (1996).
Varga (2001) found that some children of preschool age use hyperbole, which
requires understanding of figurative instead of literal meanings. They can
make outrageously false statements about their abilities (i.e., telling tall tales),
thus stimulating other children to respond by elaborating on the claims and
engendering increasing levels of laughter. Thus, early humor development
serves as an aid to "theory of mind" development, which requires knowledge
that others will not know what the humorous meaning is. Of course, for this
type of humor the presence of an audience is an important component. This
stage of humor development is not a straightforward linear process, however,
as children often can demonstrate the *form* of more complex humor types
before they understand the incongruity element. They may laugh but do not
always get the point of the riddle or joke told to them or, if they tell the riddle
or joke, they give the answer or "punch line" too soon or incorrectly. They

also may not be able to explain what is humorous about their attempt. For example, one child explained why her riddle was funny by saying, "When I tell it, mommy laughs" (Bergen, 1998).

By age 6 or 7, most children's incongruity humor is more similar to adult humor in its form although it is not as sophisticated in ideas. It may include word play, references to cognitive events, and use of multiple meanings. However, the ability to tell a joke that preserves the incongruity and meaning is a skill that continues to develop over the elementary age period. Even some adults have difficulty getting the sequence and timing of joke telling down perfectly! Another type of humor that has a sophisticated cognitive component is irony. Although children of 5-6 may show recognition that a speaker making an ironic comment does not literally believe what they have said, they do not find the remarks humorous (Harris & Pexman, 2003). Even children of age 7-10, although they can interpret ironic criticisms and compliments in comparison to literal criticisms and complements, are more able to find ironic complements humorous rather than ironic criticism (Pexman, Glenwright, Krol, & James, 2005).

Humor and Social-Emotional Development. Many theorists, researchers, and practitioners have focused their work on understanding how humor can temper emotional trauma or enhance socialization processes in adults and they have discussed many aspects of humor related to such social-emotional issues. There has also been theoretical interest in young children's humor development that is related to social and emotional dimensions. One theorist who shed light on these aspects of children's humor development was Sigmund Freud. Although primarily interested in the ways that the joking behavior of adults revealed their social-emotional coping levels, Freud (1960) also discussed the stages leading to joking behavior and the social-emotional meanings embedded in children's humor attempts. He described three stages of joking development that ultimately led to adult joking. According to Martin (1998), Freud used the term "joking" to describe this phenomenon and reserved the term "humor" to describe only the type of humor that specifically focused on the social-emotional coping strategies that humor can provide.

In Freud's analysis of joking development, he labeled the first stage as *play* (ages 2-3), which involves children repeating and elaborating on sounds, making unusual actions with objects, engaging in peek-a-boo first initiated by parents, and performing familiar actions in new ways. All of these humor-related play strategies are facilitated in social "trust" environments. Because the trust environment is so important for this humor play, it occurs primarily in close social-emotional situations, which is why a young child may react by crying if an unknown adult attempts similar behaviors.

According to Wolfenstein (1954), at about age 3 or 4, children's pretense becomes differentiated into two strands, one of which is "serious" and the other is "joking" make-believe. In serious make-believe, the real world is simulated, and children try to make their actions resemble the real world as closely as their understanding permits. For example, they will take the role of "Mom" and "cook" dinner. On the other hand, in joking make-believe, children deliberately distort reality with the intention of getting a surprise effect or a humorous response. This ability leads to the second stage of joking that Freud identified, which he called *jesting* (ages 4-6). Freud stated that the jesting behavior of young children (making exaggerated sounds and behaviors) does not intend to convey cognitive meaning; rather jests are just designed to provoke a social response, such as laughter in the "social partners." This stage is sometimes called "teasing" or "clowning." He saw this behavior as the originating point for nonsense or "comic" expression in adult humor.

The ability of the audience to respond to jesting behavior is an important part of the social interaction. Thus, jesting always requires an audience and it becomes escalated by the audience interaction. Often children who use jesting have had parents who modeled jesting behavior to them, and they began to understand the difference between these two modes of action. For example, the parent may have made deliberate mistakes, such as singing a song with the wrong words or doing some other act of "fooling" so the child learns to react to this behavior by laughing. Jesting doesn't work if the social partner (adult, sibling, or peer) does not react by being "fooled" or by elaborating the jest even further. In studies of toddler's humor expressions, the initiation of jests by parents was a commonly observed action (Bergen, 2001). For example, one parent asked his daughter to eat another item of the food on her plate (beans) but after asking twice and having the child refuse, the parent then escalated the interaction into a game by making up other delicious food names not on the plate (cake, pie, ice cream) and asking the same question. Each time the child's "no" response was accompanied by laughter. Thus, in regard to jesting behavior, there is a strong socialization element. It is possible that adults who "can't take a joke" did not have parents, siblings, or other known individuals help them learn this jesting behavior when they were young.

Freud's third stage of joking begins about age 6 but is not fully developed until about age 12 (see Bergen, 1998). He saw true joking as a means of conveying social-emotional meanings that may not be allowed expression except through a joking format. Of course, many jokes are not of a socially unacceptable type but adults often make good use of this "joking facade" (Wolfenstein, 1954) that permits the expression of emotion-laden sexual, hostile, or otherwise unacceptable meanings that could not be expressed seriously. Even by age 5 or 6 children who have older siblings or joking parents may demonstrate the social convention of "joke telling," in which they use the form of a joke or riddle without getting the point of their use for conveying unacceptable meanings. By about age 9 children begin to be adept at telling jokes correctly and, by age 12, many of their jokes have hostile and/or sexual themes similar to those common in adult humor. Younger children's humor attempts may be crude, referring to body parts, elimination, or other unacceptable topics; that is, they are usually not adept at putting them in a socially acceptable format. Although adults usually do not approve of this gross type of joking humor, it is often considered hilarious by peers and it serves to bond the peer group members. Social interactions that employ the joking façade underlie much of the humor of older children and adults, and such humor often conveys hurtful messages while still being symbolic rather than realistic (Warm, 1997). Unfortunately, as older children learn the joking format, they may begin to use it to demonstrate hostility or rejection of other children, especially if they are in a peer group that focuses on excluding other children.

Some forms of humor can be an important method of enabling individuals to gain an altered and more realistic perception of threatening social and other environmental situations. For example, humor can be used by hospital personnel to help assuage young patients' anxiety (Bergen & Gaynard, 1986; Schwekbe & Gryski, 2003), to help children cope with anxieties about their abilities (Wolfenstein, 1954), and to aid in bonding with social groups (Fine & Soucey (2005), A phenomenon known as "group glee" demonstrates that humor can be catching and engage an entire social group, engaging even toddlers or preschoolers in a bonding experience (Masellos 2003; Sherman, 1975). Young children often tell the same riddle over and over with the expectation that the hearer will laugh each time, and usually dad or mom will comply.

Various types of humor also have been studied for their particular effect on social interactions. For example, teasing is prominent in childhood social exchanges and is a type that is learned at an early age by most children. Irony, however, is more difficult to understand. Because humor development occurs with the frame of adult-child early social interactions, and shared cultural understandings, adult humor-eliciting behaviors give communication signals that help children learn what behaviors should be exhibited when social interactions occur in different social "frames." Thus, when adults engage with infants and toddlers in playful ways, they are communicating that there is a "play frame," which signals "This is play" (Bateson, 1956). Engagement within a play frame is essential for humor expression. The signals that communicate a humor frame are similar to those that identify a play frame, such as exaggerated facial expressions, higher-pitched voice, intense gaze, and smiles or open mouth (Stern, 1974). By 6 months of age, infants can distinguish play frames and respond differentially within those frames (Pien & Rothbart, 1980). From this theoretical perspective, it is vitally important that young children have both serious and playful/humorous social interactions so that they will learn to interpret these social-cultural differences and know how to respond appropriately in both types of settings. It is often the case that children who are not socially adept may have difficulty distinguishing when an interaction is playfully humorous and may not know the social signals they can use to engage in such social humor.

This perspective suggests that human capacity to become socially skilled users of humor depends on learning how to interpret and react to the metacommunication "this is humor" (Bergen, 1998). Studies of abused or neglected children often report that abused children have difficulty engaging in play and it is likely that they also do not know how to engage in socially appropriate humor events. The research examples of adult and child initiation of humor illustrate how the responses of the social partner can make a big difference in humor production and understanding. Thus, humor development can be facilitative of children's social and emotional health.

Humor Development of Children with Cognitive Gifts

Because humor development accompanies children's cognitive and social development, an area of research comparing the trajectories of humor development between typically developing and gifted children has been useful to gain insight into ways this group may be more skilled at using humor as a way of gaining mastery over their world. In addition to her study of humor development of toddlers, preschoolers, and elementary age children (Bergen, 1998/2007, 2001, 2003), Bergen also has looked in depth at the humor of children who have been identified as gifted (2004, 2009, 2015). One of the major questions related to gifted children's humor is whether they show evidence of earlier movement to the higher levels of humor discussed by Freud and by McGhee. The research evidence suggests that even by age five, many gifted children show a wide range of humor behavior and understand humor that has conceptual incongruity and levels of multiple meaning. In a study comparing types of humor displayed by typically developing children, findings showed that the types of humor displayed at age 7-9 and 10-12 differed. That is, the younger sample of typically developing children showed the pattern of humor development predicted by Freudian and Piagetian (i.e., Magee interpretation) theory (Bergen, 1998). In studies with two samples of gifted children that compared the two age levels (7-9 and 10-12), the younger gifted age groups already were exhibiting the whole range of humor types, supporting the conclusion that humor development in gifted children is accelerated (Bergen, 2012, 2015).

In the most recent study (Bergen, 2015), 65 children (34 male; 31 female; ages 8-12) identified as gifted from 3 schools in the same district were studied using the structured interview used in previous studies. They were asked about humorous TV/online shows and books and examples of funny events at home and school. The interview requires them to produce a riddle or joke, to solve riddle punch lines with hints as needed, and to rate their own sense of humor on an eighteen question Likert scale. The results replicated the Bergen (2012) study, showing that their humor development was accelerated in comparison to the typically developing sample (1998). This group of gifted children gave examples of electronic media humor, with *Sponge Bob* examples being the most often TV source; however, they also gave examples from online media such as UTube. Their book examples at both times included *Harry Potter*, but the recent group also cited *Wimpy Kid* extensively. In most examples, they cited incongruous actions, and such actions were also primary in their examples from home and school. Ove 80% of the children produced riddles or jokes. A few examples are:

Riddle/joke	Reason cited as why funny
Knock, knock, whose there? Lettuce. Lettuce (let us) in, it is cold out there.	You think it's a vegetable but the word sounds like a different word. (word play)
There were two peanuts but one was assaulted (a salted).	You hear it one way but find it means a different thing the other way. (word play)
If you are an American outside the bathroom, what are you inside? European	Because instead of European its "you're "you're a peein" (word play, incongruity, tendentious)
Mary's father had 4 kids – April, May, June. What was the other one's name? Mary	No one expects it to be Mary unless you are listening carefully (word play, incongruity)

In regard to their self-ratings of their own humor, the mean was 3.97 out of possible 4.0! They also were proficient at guessing riddle punch lines, having a 70-80% success rate after hints that helped them think about the joking answer.

The current study supported earlier results, showing that, gifted children have high ability for riddle/joke production and their riddles have not only the form but also the function of a complete riddle or joke. By age ten, many gifted children understand and express humor that is comparable in form and function to that of adults. The topics differ from adult humor, of course, since their experiential base is more limited. However, they are able appreciate satire in books and even some political cartoons. Although research shows that both gifted boys and girls have a high level of ability to comprehend and enjoy incongruous types of humor, and children of both genders rate themselves similarly as to their sense of humor on self-report scales, teachers and peers often rate gifted boys as having a higher senses of humor than gifted girls (Bergen & Jewett, 2000; Luftig & Nichols, 1999). Gifted children are similar to other children in that they find humor in many different settings, including home, school, books, and other media. However, they typically continue to be great book readers even in this electronic media age.

Humor Development in Children with Special Cognitive or Social-Emotional Needs

Research on the humor of children with special needs reports some evidence that their comprehension and production of humor shows developmental lags. In an extensive review of the humor development of children with physical illnesses, intellectual disabilities, autism and Down's syndrome, and learning/intellectual disabilities, Semrud-Clikeman and Glass (2010) generally reported that, while the earlier levels of humor (e.g., peek-a-boo, incongruous actions) did not usually show differences from controls, the types of incongruity humor that involved cartoons, riddles or jokes or other language-based humor typically had differences for these groups from controls. The children with such disabilities were less able to tell jokes and to explain why they were funny and could not understand the incongruities in the humor, although there were differences also among children with varied types of disabilities. For example, children with Down's syndrome were more responsive and initiating of humor than children with autism syndrome disabilities. The study of humor development in children who have special needs is only beginning, but it is an important area of concern.

Suggestions for Facilitating Positive Humor Development

Individuals who can use humor appropriately to understand and act effectively, to facilitate social relationships, and to manage emotions may have greater cognitive maturity, self- regulation, and perhaps, general well-being. On the other hand, those who use humor inappropriately, in hostile or excessively self-disparaging ways may affect both themselves and those with whom they interact negatively. There are many reports of teasing or other types of humor being used to disparage other children or bully them and this seems to be escalating in the present social media world. One way that adults can help children learn to deal with such behaviors is to help them have a well-developed ability to both understand and to use humor appropriately.

When adults interact in playful and humor-eliciting ways with young children, they can help them learn how to use humor as a facilitator of social interaction and determine what behaviors are appropriate to exhibit. Even infants and toddlers can learn that there is a "play frame," which signals "This is humor; this is play" and that behavior within that frame is different from behaviors in "serious" frames. Humor, almost by definition, requires social interaction, although the audience for humor differs at various ages, with parents and other caregivers being the first audience for children, and, progressively, siblings, peers, teachers, and people in other settings being involved in the audience role. Early expressions of humor require a "safe" environment in which children can take the risk of humor expression, and try out their humor attempts with a responsive audience. Of course children differ in their interest and ability to express and enjoy humor; however, almost every kindergarten or first grade child can tell a riddle if asked to do so.

An important social skill that children should learn is being able to understand when to interpret an action or a verbal comment or unusual action as "this is humor." In elementary school, often teasing of children who can't "take" a joke is a first step in their social isolation. Similarly, older children and adolescents will rate a peer who has a "sense of humor" more positively. Thus, being able to appreciate and express humor fosters social acceptance and friendship at all ages. Helping children to learn how to interpret and use humor effectively is an important part of both parents' and educators' role. Here are some suggestions for fostering positive humor development (adapted from Bergen, 2007):

1. Express appreciation for children's humor attempts, and give them opportunities to attempt humor themselves.
2. Share one's own humor attempts at home and in the classroom (even if these attempts are somewhat lame!).
3. Provide social environments that invite humorous as well as serious elaborations of learning tasks.
4. Teach and demonstrate different types of humor, such as riddling, tall tales, irony/teasing, and practice those.
5. Read humorous stories and show humorous videos with varied examples of different types of humor and discuss why they are funny.
6. Help children understand what is appropriate teasing and what is inappropriate, and empower children to find ways to respond to teasing so that it does not evolve into bullying.

CONCLUSION

The topic of humor development has many interesting dimensions and more researchers should be focusing on children's development of humor since it has the ability to enrich both their cognitive and social-emotional life. As with any ability, however, the ability to appreciate and use humor appropriately does not develop as an isolated skill. It is tied closely to biological factors, to other areas of development, and to environments that do or do not encourage it to flower. Children's humor development can be encouraged in many ways and should be considered as an important developmental area because the ability to see the humor in various situations is an effective coping mechanism useful throughout life.

REFERENCES

Aimard, P. (1992). Genese de phumour. *Devenir,* 4(3), 27-40.
Bariaud, F. (1989). Age differences in children's humor. *Journal of Children in Contemporary Society,* 20 (1-2), 15-45.

Bergen, D. (2015, July). Children's play and humor development: Gifted children's humor preferences, sense of humor, and comprehension of riddles. Paper presented at International Society of Humor Studies, San Francisco, CA.

Bergen, D. (2009). Gifted children's humor preferences, sense of humor, and comprehension of riddles. *Humor*, 22(4), 419-436.

Bergen, D. (2007) Humor as a facilitator of social competence in early childhood. In B. Spodek & O. Saracho (Eds*). Contemporary perspectives in early childhood education*. Greenwich, CT: Information Age.

Bergen, D. (2004). Humor development of gifted and typically developing children: A synthesis of present knowledge. Revue quebecoise de psychologie, Quebec, Canada: University of Quebec, 25(1), 1-21.

Bergen, D. (1998). Development of the sense of humor. In W. Ruch (Ed.), *The sense of humor: Explorations of a personality characteristic.* (pp. 329-358). Berlin: Mouton deGruyter.

Bergen, D., & Jewett, L. (2000). Teacher facilitation of learning through play and humor in early childhood and elementary/middle school classrooms. Symposium paper presented at the 16th Biennial Meeting of the International Society for the Study of Behaviour and Development, Beijing, PRC, July.

Fine, G. A., & Soucey, M. D. (2005). Joking cultures: Humor themes as social regulation in group life. *Humor-International Journal of Humor Research*, 18(1), 1-22.

Freud, S. (1960*).* Jokes and their relation to the unconscious. New York: Norton.

Harris, M. & Pexman, P. M. (2003). Children's perceptions of the social functionsof verbal irony. *Discourse Processes,* 36, 147–165.

Klein, A. (1985). Humor comprehension and humor appreciation of cognitively oriented humor: A study of kindergarten children. *Child Development,* 56, 223-235.

Luftig, R. & Nichols, M. L. (1999). An assessment of the social status and perceived personality and school traits of gifted students by non-gifted peers. *Roeper Review,* 13(3), 148-153.

Martin, R. (1998). Approaches to the sense of humor: A historical review. In W. Ruch (Ed.) The sense of humor: Explorations of a personality characteristic (pp. 15-60). Berlin: Mouton de Gruyter.

McGhee, P. E. (2002). Understanding and promoting the development of children's humor. Dubuque, IA: Kendall/Hunt.

Pexman, P. M., Glenwright, M., Krol, A., & James, T. (2005). An acquired taste: Children's perceptions of humor and teasing in verbal irony. *Discourse Processes*, 40(3), 259-288.

Piaget, J. (1962). *Play*, dreams and imitation in childhood. New York: Norton.

Pien, D. & Rothbart, M. K. (1976). Incongruity and resolution in children's humor: A reexamination. *Child Development*, 47, 966-971.

Schwekbe, S. & Gryski, C. (2003). Gravity and levity–pain and play: The child and the clown in the pediatric health care setting. In A. Klein, (Ed.). Humor in children's lives: A guidebook for practitioners (pp. 49–68). Westport, CT: Praeger.

Semrud-Clikeman and Glass (2010). The relation of humor and child development: Social, adaptive, and emotional aspects. *Journal of Child Neurology*, 000(00) 1-13, DOI: 10.1177/0883073810373144.

Sherman, L. W. (1975). An ecological study of glee in small groups of preschool children. *Child Development*, 46, 53-61.

Sinclair, A. (1996). Young children's practical deceptions and their understanding of false belief. *New Ideas in Psychology*, 14(2), 152-173.

Varga, D. (2000). Hyperbole and humor in children's language play. *Journal of Research in Childhood Education*, 14(2).142-146.

Vernon, P. A., Villani, V. C., Schermer, J. A., & Kirilovic, S. (2009). Genetic and environmental correlations between trait emotional intelligence and humor styles. *Journal of Individual Differences* 2009; Vol. 30(3):130–137.

Warm, T. R. (1997). The role of teasing in development and vice versa. *Journal of Developmental & Behavioral Pediatrics*, 18(2), 97-181.

Wolfenstein, M. (1954). *Children's humor: A psychological analysis*. Glencoe, IL: Free Press.

In: Humor   ISBN: 978-1-63484-787-2
Editor: Holly Phillips   © 2016 Nova Science Publishers, Inc.

Chapter 2

A KINDERGARTEN CLASS CLOWN: PLAY AND EMPOWERMENT MOTIVES

Eleni Loizou, EdD*
Associate Professor, Department of Education,
University of Cyprus, Nicosia, Cyprus

ABSTRACT

Humor can be a form of social power and it is socially constructed. Children produce and appreciate humor as a means of constructing, deconstructing and understanding their socio-cultural context. Specifically, kindergarteners employ humor during free play and structured activities in their classroom as a means to have fun, play, cope with and exert power, question rules, test the limits and socially empower themselves. This chapter portrays humor as a form of social empowerment and is based on the theoretical framework of the theory of the Absurd and the Empowerment theory (Loizou, 2005). Data from a single case study is described to highlight how a kindergartener, a boy class clown, employs humor within his early childhood setting and how he becomes socially empowered. The research questions explored are: "What type of humor does a boy class clown, a kindergartner, produce in his early childhood classroom?" "Is this type of humor differentiated

* Corresponding author: Eleni Loizou, EdD. Associate Professor, Department of Education, University of Cyprus, P.O. Box 20537, 1678 Nicosia, Cyprus. Tel: +357-22 892950, Fax: +357-22 894487, e-mail: eloizou@ucy.ac.cy.

according to the classroom context?" and "What are his social motives for producing humor?"

Data collection involved participant observations of play and structured activities, semi structured interviews with the children and the teachers, and document review. Specific examples of observational anecdotes and statements are used to explore each research question and highlight the types of humor produced as well as the correlation with social empowerment. The chapter supports the Theory of the Absurd and the Empowerment theory as a framework of unfolding the clowning behaviors of a kindergartener and provides a positive way of considering clowning during the early childhood years highlighting its importance to play and social empowerment.

INTRODUCTION

The aim of this chapter is to unfold the humorous behaviors of a young child, who has been identified by his teachers as the "class clown," in order to describe how class clowns produce humor and for what social reasons they do so through the lens of the Theory of the Absurd and the Empowerment theory (Loizou, 2005). More specifically, with the use of a case study, the humorous behaviors of a boy kindergartener will be examined as exhibited in his natural setting and during his every day kindergarten activities. In particular, we seek to deconstruct these humorous behaviors and pinpoint the social motives entailed in them.

Humor Literature

Humor is a complex multidimensional phenomenon hard to define and can be interpreted in multiple ways. Nevertheless, there have been attempts to define and consider the ways people produce and/or appreciate humor unfolding a number of theories such as the Superiority theory; when we laugh at someone's misfortune, the Relief theory; when we laugh because of overcoming a stressful moment, and the Incongruity theory; when we laugh at the mismatch of existing schemata. In addition, multiple studies (Banas et al., 2010, Booth-Butterfield et al. 2007, Murdock & Ganim 1993, Hoicka & Akhtar, 2012) have examined humor and how it affects our health, communication among people and cultures, advertising, education, psychology, linguistics, etc. Research has also attempted to deconstruct children's humorous behaviors, to understand how and why children produce humor. McGhee has lead the way in framing young children's (2-7 years) humor development. Specifically, McGhee (1979) talks about four stages through which young children's humor unfolds, and these are: a. Incongruous actions towards objects, b. Incongruous labeling of objects and events, c. Conceptual incongruity and d. Multiple meanings. His work on children's humor is focused on the view of humor as an incongruity and he highlights the importance of cognitive development in being able to produce and appreciate humor (Bergen 2008; Lyons & Fitzgerald 2004).

We choose to view humor as a social phenomenon which happens between at least two persons and involves smiles and/or laughter. Loizou (2002) has also developed a framework with which she explores the production and appreciation of humor of infants, the Theory of the Absurd and the Empowerment Theory. Her theoretical framework draws from the Incongruity and the Superiority Theory suggesting that infants produce and appreciate humor and in their attempts they show both their cognitive and social development. Specifically, through the Theory of the Absurd, three sub-categories suggest how children produce and appreciate humor and these include: a. Funny Gestures/Positions/Sounds/Words, b. Incongruous use of materials and c. Incongruous actions. In reference to the Empowerment theory two sub-categories exist: a. Spontaneous- intentional violation of expectation; when children spontaneously and purposefully violate the expectations of their caregivers and b. Responsive-intentional violation of expectation; when children violate the expectations of their caregivers as a result of a positive response they get for their actions. Loizou has examined the specific scientific framework with older children and in different aspects of humor involvement such as visual and verbal appreciation and production (Loizou, 2006, Loizou, 2011, Loizou et al. 2011). The current work is an attempt to examine children's clowning through the lens of the above mentioned theoretical framework within an early childhood setting and during the daily activities of a child labeled as the "class clown." We assume that such a humorous space, that of clowning, entails some form of incongruity with empowerment experiences, agreeing with Hobday-Kusch and McVittie (2002) that humor can be "a deliberate way to shift power relations within a social context" (p. 202).

Class Clown Literature

There are three trends in the humor literature focusing on class clowns. Firstly, studies (mostly psychological) explore the different types of class clowns and some move on to the analysis of their behavior. Secondly, class clown behaviors are examined in reference to their development and the impact of their behavior on their learning, teaching and classroom climate. Thirdly, such studies mainly focus on elementary school children and/or older.

Damico and Purkey (1976, 1978), examined class clowns among middle school students and with the use of sociometric data they distinguished among two types of class clowns. These types include: a. the popular group leader, who is the creative, social and popular child and b. the isolate, who is the isolated, unpopular child who mainly makes fun of others. Moreover, Fine (1983) analyzes specific typologies of people who use humor and describes their profile. The Fool is the person who is "a figure of fun…who is intellectually insufficient" (p. 161); the Clown who is "a performer as in circuses" (p. 162), the Joker who "has a humorous remark for all occasions" (p. 163) and the Comedian who aims at making other people laugh.

Ruch, Platt and Hofmann (2014) employed a variable-centered approach rather than a type concept one, to the study of class clowns. Specifically, they have investigated the character strengths of class clowns and developed dimensions of class clown behaviors. These included the "identified class clown," the "comic talent," the "rule breaker" and" subversive joker." These dimensions were then examined with specific character and leadership strengths were correlated with the first two types of class clowns. This work proposes that there are different types of class clowns and teachers should provide different attention to them.

Furthermore, there is a number of studies which investigate both the types and functions of humor production and particularly research which makes the connection between the production of humor and the social functions involved. Norrick and Klein (2008) examine class clowning, humorous production, as forms of disruptive behavior in the elementary classroom and endeavor in understanding the reasons behind such behaviors. Their findings suggest that humorous disruptions, as employed by class clowns, help children develop their unique identity and highlight their class personality within an impersonal elementary school classroom.

A number of other studies (Fine, 1977; Sletta and Sobstad, 1993; Klein and Kuiper, 2006; Huuki, Manniner, and Sunnari, 2010; Hobday-Kusch and McVittie, 2002) examined how humor can affect the development of group culture and how it can be used to influence the social status of children. Such studies explicate that children who employ humor with their peers, tend to also exhibit aggressive behavior towards them and that the line between playfulness and bullying is thin. "Humor flowers from interpersonal relationships" (Ziv, 2010, p. 12) thus humor production is closely related to the formation of relationships, and can have an impact, positive and/or negative, on people within a group, a community or the society. Ziv (2010) describes the social functions of humor for the individual in a group. He asserts that humor can be the tool we, as humans, utilize to fulfill our need to belong, to be affiliated to a number of groups, and to obtain status within these groups. From another perspective, equally important, Fine (1983) supports that for humor experiences to be lived there is a need for an existing social relationship and that humor is often part of society and culture concluding that it is socially regulated (Fine, 1983).

The educational setting of a classroom is a context in which children attempt to develop relationships and to assert their social status, with their peers and teachers. Šeďová (2013) analyzed the humorous written texts of 12-15 year olds which were addressed to their teachers as a way to examine the type of humor produced and its functions. Her results suggest that children in their writings present three types of teachers (comical, duped and humorous) and that these refer to different social functions (solidarity, power and needs). Šeďová (2013) concludes that humor provides opportunities for students to react to teacher power and facilitates their independence.

The aim of this chapter to add to the existing literature by investigating class clowning within an early childhood setting focusing on the behaviors of a kindergartener class clown. We are defining class clown as the child who is producing a lot of humorous acts/events during their daily activities to make his/her peers smile and/or laugh. So, the research questions explored are:

1. What type of humor does a boy class clown, a kindergartener, produce in his early childhood classroom?
    a. Is this type of humor differentiated according to the classroom context?
2. What are his social motives for producing humor?

We choose to consider humor as a means which young children employ in order to form their social identity and to be playful within their environment, with their peers and teachers.

METHODOLOGY

This is a qualitative study which pursues the case study methodology seeking to perform an in depth examination of "the social interaction and the construction of meaning in situ" (Chadderton & Torrance, 2011, p. 53); the humorous experiences of a boy class clown within his early childhood setting.

Participants

The participants of this study included all of the children in a kindergarten classroom and their two teachers. More specifically we focus on Erik, the identified by his teachers' "class clown," who was five and a half years old. He had been attending the specific school for two years and had the same peers for the same amount of time. He is the youngest in a family of two, has a 10 year old sister, and his parents were in the process of divorcing during the time of the data collection. The two teachers of the classroom were between the ages of 24-29 at the time and they both have a Bachelors degree in Early Childhood Education and a Masters degree in the field of Education. They had both been teaching in the specific school for at least two years.

Data Collection

The data collection methods included: participant observations, a focus group interview with the class clown and his friends, semi-structured interviews with his teachers and document review. Data was collected for two weeks from the beginning until the end of the day (7.30 am-15.30 pm) and the children were observed during their daily activities and the humorous events that the class clown produced were recorded. For each event, the description of the event, the participants, the context and its outcome were noted. Then a week later the teachers and a group of children (4 children) that the class clown had chosen as his best friends were interviewed. In both cases the aim was to unfold the teachers' and children's experiences with the class clown and see how they were reacting to his humorous productions. The teachers during the interview provided examples of situations where Erik was producing humor and reflected on the different ways they dealt with it. During the focus group discussion the children were involved in commenting on some funny pictures and then they were asked to consider the child who makes them laugh most in the classroom and share their experiences and specific humorous events with the "class clown." Finally, document review involved the two developmental summaries of Erik as prepared by his teachers each semester. These documents described his progress in all areas of development as well as his learning in different content areas with the use of specific anecdotes drawn from his daily activities and interactions in the classroom.

School Context-Curriculum

The school is the first and only University-based school of the country and during the time of the data collection had been in its third year of existence. The school's pedagogical philosophy is based on the framework of a learning community and it is especially focusing on children's individual needs, rights and participation opportunities employing the project approach as a means to create a space where children become agents of their learning and development. The school has three child care, two preschool and one kindergarten classrooms. It serves up to 105 children, there are two teachers in each classroom and there is a principal on site.

The daily schedule includes: Free activities, breakfast, circle time, free play outdoors, fruit time, circle time, quiet activities. During free and quiet activities, the children are involved in play and playful activities which are set in learning centers and they are free to choose where to go, what and whom to play with. During circle time there is a set lesson plan by the teacher (e.g., a story to be read, a mathematical skill/concept to develop) and usually there is a discussion while sitting in a circle and then the children go in their groups to work.

Data Analysis

The Theory of the Absurd and the Empowerment theory with their subcategories were applied as the main data analysis tool for the humorous productions of the class clown. In reference to the social motives involved in the production of humor the different humorous events were read and re-read and common themes were grouped. Table 1 provides the details of the data analysis showing the humorous production categories, the type of humor produced, as well as the social motives that were uncovered in the class clown's humorous behavior.

Table 1. Type of humor production and social motives

Type of Humor Production	Social Motives
Theory of the Absurd • Incongruous actions: movement and gestures • Incongruous use of materials • Humorous use of language	*Play oriented motives* a. join in a play activity b. respond to play invitations c. create play invitations d. deal with a play rejection e. create a playful moment
The Empowerment theory • Purposeful violation of teacher expectations	*Empowerment seeking motives* • challenge the teaching moment • create a pleasurable moment • preserve social humorous status

FINDINGS

With the use of data from the multiple sources Erik's humorous personality is unfolded. Through his developmental summaries Erik is described as a child who is actively involved in the classroom activities, who initiates different games and invites other children to follow him. He mostly enjoys pretend play taking on different roles and suggesting different scenarios (e.g., pretends to be a rabbit running fast in the classroom pretends to be a teacher and with a serious facial expression pretends to be writing on the board). Observational data show how Erik is involved in humorous productions within the framework of the Theory of the Absurd and the Empowerment theory. He is acting incongruously using mainly movements and gestures, he is incongruously using materials, mainly classroom toys, and he is playing with language, finding the double meaning in words, creating rhyming and purposefully providing wrong answers. In reference to the Empowerment theory he is seen to purposefully violate the expectations of his teachers.

Details of Type of Humor Production

Theory of the Absurd

Incongruous Actions
The observations of Erik show how he was involved in multiple humorous events where he was acting incongruously either using gestures or movements; thus jumping, running in the classroom, doing gymnastics in the classroom, laying on the floor, moving his hands or feet very fast or very slowly, dragging himself on the floor, etc. A characteristic example of such behavior is highlighted in the following humorous episode:

> The children are sitting on their chairs in the circle. Erik gets up and moves in front of his peers and starts dancing, moving his body back and forth. The children watch him and laugh.

Incongruous Use of Materials
Moreover, his humor production included the incongruous use of materials. For example he was observed to use a board game as a hat or a pillow, to use kitchen vegetables as bombs, to place a hat on his genitals, to pretend to melt crayons in a bowl at the kitchen. The following humorous episode is an example where he is misplacing a sticker:

> Erik goes to the bathroom and places a sticker on his ear and returns to the classroom walking around showing off his sticker.

Language Play
In his developmental summaries his teachers comment on his advanced linguistic abilities highlighting on his skill to play with words (e.g., using the Cypriot dialect when asked to find words that rhyme), to produce rhyme and create words as a response to structured activities. Moreover, data from observations show how Erik endorses sounds, words, language in general as a means to create humor. He is playing with the double meaning of words, creating rhyming, telling jokes, uses inappropriate words in his singing, and in communicating with his friends, (e.g., poop, bra). A lot of his language play involves inappropriate words within the scatology form and involves sexual insinuations. The humorous event that follows is a characteristic example of him playing with language, where he is trying to create a rhyme including words that make some sexual insinuation.

While the children are getting together at the circle to listen to a story Erik is singing a song changing the verse and says "Andrew is making fun of others but he lost his underwear and walks around naked"

The Empowerment Theory

Erik was observed to use humor in order to violate the expectations of his teachers, most frequently during circle time, but at other contexts as well. The following episodes show how he purposefully violates his teachers' expectations and directions:

> The children are standing up saying their prayer and Erik is sitting on his chair banging loudly his feet on the floor.

> The teacher asks Erik to go get a sheet of paper and when he returns to sit on his chair he starts dancing stamping his feet on the floor. A child sitting next to him copies his action.

Erik is aware of the rules, routines and the expectations within his classroom, the discursive practices and purposefully finds ways to react to them by creating humorous events.

Social Motives behind the Humorous Production

In this section, the social motives involved in the different humorous events that Erik produced will be elaborated. These social motives include two general categories: a. Play oriented and b. Empowerment seeking motives. Various humorous episodes will be presented to pinpoint the social aspects involved in his attempt to produce humor and at the same time the content of the humor will be highlighted. Moreover, through the following episodes it will be shown that Erik produced humor that was addressed to a single peer/ teacher, a group of peers and/or the whole class.

Play Oriented Motives

Erik was observed to produce humor, in multiple ways, as a means to participate in play. More, specifically the data analysis led to specific subcategories within his general social motive which was play and these were: a. to join a play activity, b. to respond to play invitations, c. to create play invitations, d. to deal with a play rejection and e. to create a playful moment. These will be further explained and supported with specific humorous episodes.

Join in a Play Activity

Erik is engineering humor in different ways in order to join in a play activity with a peer or a group of peers. He is using humor as a play cue to get permission to become part of a play activity.

> Erik moves towards the library area where one of his friends is and sis on him. They both start laughing.

The specific example shows how Erik focuses on finding a way to join in play with a specific friend and he is acting incongruously, using his whole body, in order to get play permission/approval.

Respond to Play Invitations

Another play oriented category involves the way Erik responded to play invitations from his peers. In the following episodes Erik is being humorous, acting incongruously, and employing scatology, as a means of responding to the play invitations by his peers.

> One of his classmates enters the classroom and holds a hat with a green pig and she immediately goes to Erik to show him her hat. Erik shouts loudly with a funny voice "here is an angry pig, lets shoot it" and he begins to pretend to shoot the girl. When he is done he says "now it's diarrhea." Two other boys who were there and saw the incident laugh.

> Two children are at the library area and they call Erik. "Erik? Erik?" Erik goes close to them and with a funny voice says "what do you want?" putting his hands on his waist. All three children begin to laugh.

It is evident how he easily and immediately constructs verbal and/or bodily humor to respond to his peers' play invitations and become part of the group.

Deal with Play Rejection

Erik uses humor as a way to deal with play rejection. In the following episode he is acting again incongruously, pretending to sing an adult English song, in order to deal with a play rejection from a group of children.

> Erik goes to a group of girls and asks to join in their play. The girls ignore him and he leaves. While moving away he starts to sing out loud

"Wish you" and falls down, uses his hands to pretend he is playing the guitar. Two of his close friends see him and burst into laughing.

Create Play Invitations

Erik other than using humor to accept play offers, he is also inviting a peer or a group of peers in play. In the following episodes he is acting incongruously using his body and specific movements, as an attempt to invite his peers to play.

Erik gets on the floor and begins to make pushups with one hand, counting out loud. The children do not pay any attention to him, at one point a friend of his sees him and goes close to him and they begin to dance in front of everybody laughing.

Erik starts doing pushups in the middle of the class saying "here is my big bike" and checks to see if the children are looking at him. The children, who are at the library, smile and call him to go there…

Moreover, there are specific episodes where he is incongruously using play materials and specific language taking advantage of the common understanding, the football discourse; he has with a group of peers as a way to invite them to play.

Erik goes to the kitchen center and takes a green pepper and says out loud with a funny voice "Omonoia [the name of a football team] like a pepper [the color of the specific team is green], ha ha ha." He then begins to run in the classroom singing loudly the name of his football team "Apoel, Apoel." All of the children see him and laugh

Erik is using his body incongruously, doing pushups in the middle of the classroom as a way to draw attention from his classmates, and most of the times he succeeds since children turn look at him, laugh and join him. This data is supported by information in his developmental summaries where his teachers under the social development area state "most of the times, Erik is the child who starts a game and invites other children to follow him."

Create a Playful Moment

There were multiple events that took place during times when children were not necessarily involved in a fun, playful situation. For example, children had to follow specific rules, stay on line, and wait for everyone to finish eating so Erik used materials and language incongruously in order to create playful moments for himself and his peers.

> Erik is at the table with a group of children having his breakfast. He begins to take his container and throw it up in the air trying to catch it. He repeats this for many times and the children in his table laugh and begin to try and catch it before he does.

> Erik is on the line to walk back to their classroom from the dining area. He begins to tickle the child in front of him, the child laughs out loud, and Erik goes on to say: "Crazy stuff and poop" and they both laugh.

> Erik takes the container of a friend at the breakfast table and tells everyone that it is a mouse and moves it continuously. The child laughs and then they all repeat the same action moving their own containers on the table. Then Erik takes his own container and invites all of the children to put each one on top of the other. They all do so...

In the above examples Erik used humor in order to turn a boring and serious moment into a fun and playful one for all of them. Moreover, data from his developmental summaries, as noted by his teachers, further support that he creates a fun playful atmosphere in the classroom. The following anecdote clearly supports such behavior:

> Erik decides to dance to a famous song "Evdokia" creating enthusiasm and fun for all children who begin to clap to the rhythm of the song. After he sets the stage, he invites other children to dance as well and the classroom is turned into a "dancing floor" for a while.

Empowerment Seeking Motives

Erik produced humor, acting incongruously and/or violating his teachers' expectations, creating playful and pleasurable moments in the classroom as a means to empower himself and preserve his social status.

Violating Teacher Expectations
On another level Erik is involved in humorous events, where he is purposefully violating the expectations of his teachers, especially during circle time. These violations refer to either the content of the discussion or the rules that exist during the specific time period.

The teacher asks the children about the parents of a baby prince. Erik raises his hand and says "Vasilitzia" (the name of a flower in Greek which sounds the same as queen). The children listen to him and laugh.

While the teacher is reading a story Erik gets up to go to the bathroom. He takes very slow steps and when the teacher asks him what he is doing, he responds "I am an astronaut and I moving slowly because I hover" and laughs.

Creating Pleasure
Erik is finding ways to make fun of what is being discussed in the group by responding in unexpected and sometimes inappropriate ways. In order to make a teachable moment more playful and fun he plays with the mismatch of ideas and exaggerates.

The teacher reads the title of a book by Triviza (literary meaning with three breasts). The teacher repeats the name of the author to all of the children and Erik immediately says "he has three breasts" and all of the children laugh.

During one of the structured activities the teacher asked "why can we not see the sun with our eyes" and Erik replies "because we will turn black like a burnt toast" and the children laugh.

Preserve Humor Social Status
Moreover, Erik attempts to create pleasurable, playful moments as a way of feeling empowered and preserving his social humor status, that of the clown performer. He is seeking the reaction and group laughter as a means to feel good about himself and further support his identity as a humorous performer. The following humorous events provide examples of this humorous cycle, where he is violating his teachers' expectations, creating a pleasurable moment and at the same time upgrading his social status in the group.

A new child arrived in the classroom and the teacher is playing a game with all of them to get to know each other. All of the children are expected to get up and say their name and something they like. While all of the other children are saying they love their parents, they like being with their friends, going to school, Erik with excitement and exaggeration says "I am Erik and I like puzzles a loooooooooooooooooot" Everyone laughs.

There is a discussion about the color blue and the teacher asks the children to tell her items which have the color blue. A girl comments that someone's eyes might be blue and Erik immediately comments with a serious tone in his voice "no he is black eyed" and then laughs, then repeats the comment and other children laugh as well.

The teacher tells the children how she spent her weekend and how she slept late on Saturday night. Erik immediately lays on the floor and pretends to be sleeping. The children laugh.

Most of the humorous episodes noted include the peers Erik had invited, as his best friends for the focus group interview. It is clear that there is a group of children he interacts with more often and with whom he has multiple humorous interactions, performing for them or involving them in his humorous acts. This is further supported through his developmental summaries where his teachers highlight his leadership skills, how other children ask for his help, how they frequently follow him and copy his actions.

Classroom Context Enables Specific Humorous Productions

Most of Erik's humorous production took place during the morning Free Activities time (N = 51), a time when children are free to move from one learning center to another and they can be involved in free and/or structured play. The circle time, when children sit in a circle on their chairs and they usually have a subject to discuss or explore, with their teacher leading the activity, was the one that had the second most frequent humorous events (N = 17). Finally, during the non teaching contexts, those of breakfast and fruit times the frequency of his humorous production was N = 12.

The social motives of Erik as they arise from his humorous productions, were differentiated according to the context during which they were taking place. During the context of Free Activities, where a different set of rules, expectations and routines existed in both children's and teachers' minds, the social motive was directly related to play. So, humor as a form of play invitations and/or rejections are more frequently noted during Free Activities because this context is prone to such behaviors. Thus, the data drawn from this specific case study allow us to consider that humorous behavior is context related (see Table 2).

Peersand Teachers Comment on Erik's Humorous Production

During the focus group interview the four children Erik choose to invite as his best friends agreed that it was Erik who made them laugh most during the day. Then each one shared personal humorous events they had experienced with Erik, either being part of them or just appreciating them.

Once he used his fingers to put horns on us, another time he was dancing ballet, another time I gave him an orange and he was moving his hands and body back and forth

A third joke was when he was sitting on the chair and he was pretending it was a horse saying "horsey hop hop hop, horsey hop hop hop"

Another time he was telling us that the cow farts, ha ha ha, The cow that grazes diarrhea, ha ha ha.

As seen from his peers' comments Erik was an accepted humorous performer who produced humor through incongruous actions, movements and gestures, as well as humor with language, mainly scatology. The children describe these humorous events in order to support their idea that Erik was the peer who made them laugh most, thus affirming the observation notes, of him having the role of the class clown performer. Two children specifically said:

I like it a lot when he makes jokes, I laugh a lot.
He is a really funny friend

His teachers, through the interview, also add to the above information provided by Erik's peers by affirming that he produces a lot of humor, makes the other children laugh, and define him as the "class clown." They specifically comment on how in his production of humor he mainly uses humorous gestures and movements and that the second most frequent means of humor production is language play. They describe him as social, powerful and a leader explaining that all of the children follow him. Also, they comment on how easily the other children laugh at all of his humorous acts and sometimes copy his actions. Finally, they admit that there are times that they laugh along with what he does and mainly what he says but once he gets out of hand, for example deviating too much from the expected behavior (e.g., inappropriate language use), they ask him to stop.

DISCUSSION

The Theory of the Absurd and the Empowerment theory have been an excellent framework through which we can interpret a kindergartener's clowning productions. Specifically, it has been illustrated that a kindergartener class clown is a child who uses incongruous actions, more specifically he is being humorous with his body, uses a lot of gestures and facial expressions to produce humor. He is putting on a clowning act where he endorses his body, posture, gestures and voice to produce humor. Also, he uses materials and toys incongruously to further enrich his performances. Through the same lens, he takes the role of a comedian performer where he seizes language as a tool to create humor through scatology and/or highlights the multiple meanings of words. We can thus frame part of his clowning within the Theory of the Absurd (Loizou, 2005) because he is acting incongruously in different ways. Additionally, multiple observations suggest that Erik is purposefully violating his teachers' expectations placing this kind of humor within the framework of the Empowerment theory.

Table 2. Social motives according to the classroom context

Classroom Context	Social Motives
Free Activities	Mainly play oriented
Circle Time	Mainly empowerment oriented
Non Teaching Times: breakfast, fruit and lunch time	A combination of play and empowerment oriented motives

Clowning as exhibited by this kindergartener seems to be differentiated with most literature which examines older children's clowning. The social motives of Erik's clowning behaviors are framed within two different pillars. He employed humor as a way to fulfill his play needs and secondly as a way to strengthen his social status and power in the classroom.

Play Motives

Play time in an early childhood setting is a context which entails the use of materials, toys, specific rules to be followed, peer interaction, play invitations and rejections, flexibility, fun and learning. Thus it is a context during which children act, react and negotiate in order to find their way and position in the classroom community and specific culture. They all utilize different ways and skills in order to become active members of this community, have fun and learn. So clowning, as examined in this study, has been a means by which this kindergarten boy managed to find his way in his play community, deal with relationships and play having fun. Consequently we identify clowning as a social tool which children can utilize in order to become members of a play community, overcome specific difficult moments and take ownership of this time and space as well as relationships. The use of humor, clowning, as unfolded through this case study can be considered as "a process of play cues and play returns…" (Andrews, 2012, p. 145). More specifically, Erik used humor as a " 'play cue,' the expressed intention to play" (Else, 2009, p. 13) as a way to invite peers to play and/or accept play offers. These play cues as suggested by Else (2009), in unfolding the cycle of play, can take different forms, can be verbal and/or physical with or without materials or toys. These are the different ways Erik produced humor as a means to create a play space with his peers. It is no surprise to see this form of communication taking place between young children since as it is suggested by ethologists, who scientifically study the behavior of animals, "the oldest play signals in humans are smiling and laughing" (Morreal, 2013, p. 14). Within these play motives, Erik was also involved in turning "boring" experiences into playful ones. He was initiating humor as a way to transform an uninteresting experience into a playful one, giving joy and pleasure to himself and his peers. Ziv (2010) eloquently states that "the desire to transmit humor is one of the characteristics of man, who is not only a social animal but also a pleasure seeking one" p. 12.

Empowerment Motives

On another level, data shows how Erik put on clowning performances as way to be empowered. These humorous events directly relate to the Empowerment theory Loizou (2005). More specifically, these clowning behaviors are framed under the umbrella of violating the expectations of his teachers. Erik serves as a classroom humor culture creator. He develops the playful humorous culture of the classroom while purposefully violating the expectations of the teachers, by commenting and responding to their questions in the most unexpected and certainly humorous ways.

Loizou (2007) explored the humorous productions of two infants and suggests that such experiences provided "a social context that gave them the opportunity to learn about themselves as social beings and their social power in the environment" (p. 204). Erik already has an understanding of himself as a social agent and he is purposefully being humorous in order to assert this status. He is using humor as his social power to play with the seriousness of the moment, "creating an atmosphere of enjoyment," "reflecting the views of the group with regard to external factors" and "absorbing punishment," if any and in this way he, as the "humorist child obtains status in the group" (Ziv, 2010 p. 13). Hobday-Kusch and McVittie, (2002) examined the conversation and non-verbal communications of two boy class clowns (first and second grade) and suggest that "perhaps to overcome feelings of boredom or disconnectedness, they initiated humor to take charge of given situations to get attention" (p. 204) quite similar to Erik's humorous productions. Children seem to be employing humor within their school context as a means to "test discursive practices... [and thus] "negotiate power in their classroom community" (Hobday-Kusch & McVittie, 2002, p. 208).

Moreover, Meeus and Mahieu (2009) have looked at students' written texts which described their humorous experiences with their teachers and unfolded several reasons which explain their humorous production. In particular, they suggest that children use humor in order to a. celebrate a special day/event at school, b. rebel against strict teachers, c. misbehave, react to teachers' inability to set boundaries, d. create positive atmosphere in the classroom. The last one, creating positive atmosphere, was the most frequent one and was an attempt to create fun and pleasure, quite similar to Erik's attempts of humorous productions. More specifically, Erik's humorous productions were playfully violating the expectations of his teachers as a means to create pleasure in the group and at the same time this helped him "climb the ladder of social hierarchy" (Ziv, 2010 p. 13).

So another perspective taken on the clowning of kindergarten children would be the emphasis on their efforts to create pleasure, within their group, through a play space. Mannell and McMahon (1982) who have studied the types of humorous experiences of university students suggest that "humor is a shared form of playfulness and an ingredient in many social encounters" (p. 152) which is what we are seeing for the clowning of this specific kindergartener.

CONCLUSION

This chapter asserts that humor can be a means of positive communication and social interaction within an early childhood setting. The specific case study negates other research which has asserted clowning as a form of expressing hostility and/or being aggressive with their peers. An early childhood setting which provides the space and time for children to be independent, to be active agents of their experiences, which believes in their abilities and is flexible with rules can provide the necessary milieu in which children produce humor in the most positive ways for themselves and their peers. Loizou, (2008) provides a resume of her humor studies and asserts that the Theory of the Absurd and the Empowerment theory "can be acknowledged as a general paradigm of children's humor theories" (p. 208), a statement which is further supported in this work with the case study of a class clown. Class clowning is placed within the framework of the two theories and highlights once again the socio-cognitive plane in which humor of young children is manifested. Clowning through the framework of the Theory of the Absurd and the Empowerment theory affirms that it is a playful act performed for a peer or a group of peers and based on the established relationships, it strengthens the child's agency and social status in the classroom.

ACKNOWLEDGMENTS

The author wishes to thank her graduate students, Katerina Hadjittoouli and Angelina Asimenou, for their contribution to the data collection of this chapter.

REFERENCES

Andrews, M. (2012). Exploring play for early childhood studies. Sage: London, UK.

Banas, J. A., Dunbar, N., Rodriguez, D. and Liu, S. J. (2011). A Review of Humor in Educational Settings: Four Decades of Research. *Communication Education*, 60(1), 115-144.

Bergen, D. (2008). Humour. Encyclopedia of Infant and Early Childhood *Development*, 96-106.

Booth-Butterfield, M., Booth-Butterfield, S., and Wanzer, M. B. (2007). Funny students cope better: Patterns of humor enactment and coping effectiveness. *Communication Quarterly*, 55(3), 299-315.

Chadderton, C., and Torrance, H. (2011). Case Study. In: B. Somekh and C. Lewin (Eds.) *Theory and Methods in Social Research* (2nd ed.). Los Angeles: Sage.

Damico, S.B., and Purkey, W.W. (1976). The class clown phenomenon among middle school students. Paper Presented at the Annual Meeting of the American Educational Research Association, San Francisco: US.

Damico, S.B., and Purkey, W.W. (1978). Class clowns: a study of middle school students. *American Educational Research Journal* 15, 391-398.

Else, P. (2009). Value of play. Continuum International Publishing Group.

Fine, G. A. (1983). Sociological approaches to the study of humor. In: P.E. McGhee and J. H. Goldstein (Eds.), *Handbook of humor research*, (pp. 159-181) New York: Springer-Verlag.

Fine, G.A. (1977). Humor in situ: the role of humor in small group culture. In: A. J. Chapman and H.C. Foot (Eds.), *It's a funny thing, humor* (pp. 315-318). Oxford: Pergamon Press.

Hobday-Kusch, J., and McVittie, J. (2002). Just Clowning around: Classroom perspectives on children's humor. *Canadian Journal of Education*, 27 (2/3), 195-210.

Hoicka, E. and Akhtar, N. (2012). Early humor production. *British Journal of Developmental Psychology*, 30(4), 586-603.

Huuki, T., S. Manninen, and Sunnari V. (2010). Humour as a Resource and Strategy for Boys to Gain Status in the Field of Informal School. *Gender and Education*, 22(4), 369-383.

Klein, D. N., and Kuiper, N. A. (2006). Humor styles, peer relationships, and bullying in middle childhood. *HUMOR: International Journal of Humor Research*, 19(4), 4383-404.

Loizou, E. (2002). Humorous Minds and Humorous Bodies: Humor within the social context of an infant child care setting (Unpublished doctoral dissertation), Teachers College-Columbia University, New York.

Loizou, E. (2005). Infant Humor: the Theory of the Absurd and the Empowerment Theory. *International Journal of Early Years Education*, 13(1), 43-53.

Loizou, E. (2006). Young children's explanation of pictorial humor. *Early Childhood Education Journal*, 33(6), 425-431.

Loizou, E. (2007). Humor as a means of regulating one's social self: two infants with unique humorous personas. *Early Child Development and Care*, 177(2), 195-205.

Loizou, E. (2008). Children's humor: A revised theoretical framework. In: P.G. Grotewell and Y.R. Burton (Eds.), Early Childhood Education. *Issues and Developments*. (pp. 189-211). NY: Nova Science Publishers.

Loizou, E. (2011). Disposable cameras, humor and children's abilities. *Contemporary Issues in Early Childhood*, 12(2), 148-162.

Loizou, E., Kyriakides, E., and Hadjicharalambous, M. (2011). Constructing stories in kindergarten: children's knowledge of genre. In: *European Early Childhood Education Research Journal*, 19(1), 63-77.

Lyons, V., and Fitzgerald, M. (2004). Humor in autism and Asperger syndrome. *Journal of Autism and Developmental Disorders*, 34(5), 521-531.

Mannell, R.C., and McMahon, L. (1982). Humor as play: Its relationship to psychological well-being during the course of a day. *Leisure Sciences*, 5 (2), 143-155.

McGhee, P.E. (1979). Humor its origin and development. San Florencesisco: Freeman.

Meeus, W., and Mahieu, P. (2009). You Can See the Funny Side, Can't You? Pupil Humour with the Teacher as Target. *Educational Studies*, 3(5), 553-560.

Morreall, J. (2013). Philosophy of Humor. *The Stanford Encyclopedia of Philosophy*. Edward N. Zalta (ed.), Retrieved from http://plato.stanford.edu/archives/spr2013/entries/humor/.

Murdlock, M.C. and Ganim, R.M. (1993). Creativity and humor: Integration and Incongruity. *Journal of Creative Behavior*, 27(1), 57-70.

Norrick, N. R., and Klein, J. (2008). Class Clowns: Talking out of turn with an orientation toward humor. *Lodz Papers in Pragmatics 4.1. Special Issue on Humor: 83-107.*

Ruch, W. P., T. and Hofmann, J. (2014). The character strengths of class clowns. *Frontiers in Psychology*, 5, 1-12.

Šeďová, K. (2013). Pupils' humour directed at teachers: its types and Functions. *Educational Studies*, 39(5), 522-534.

Sletta, O., and Sobstad, F. (1993). Social competence and humor in preschool and school aged children. *Paper presented at the Biennial Meeting of the Society for Research in Child Development* (60th, NewOrleans, LA, March 25-28).

Ziv, A. (2010). The Social function of humor in interpersonal relationships. *Society*, 47, 11-18.

BIOGRAPHICAL SKETCH

Name: **Eleni Loizou**
Affiliation: University of Cyprus
Education:
Ed.D, Curriculum and Teaching- Early Childhood Education.
May 2002-Columbia University - Teachers College, New York, USA
MA, Early Childhood Education, July 1997- University of Hartford, Hartford, CT, USA
BA, Pre-School Education, June 1996-University of Cyprus, Nicosia, Cyprus
Address:
University of Cyprus, P.O. Box 20537, 1678 Nicosia, Cyprus
Email: eloizou@ucy.ac.cy

Research and Professional Experience:

Dr. Loizou has been involved in multiple research projects as a regional principal investigator for Comenius Multilateral Projects, as a partner for other European projects, as a research associate for bilateral co-operations and as a principal investigator for specific Early Childhood research programs. She has conducted multiple research projects at her Early

Childhood Research Laboratory (EENA-http://www2.ucy.ac.cy/ eena/index.html) touching upon an array of subjects within the early childhood field (e.g., Fall 2012. *Giving children a voice: their understanding and suggestions of play and learning*, Summer 2011. *Play-Stories*.

Spring 2011. *Once upon a time...Children's storytelling,* Fall 2009 and Spring 2010. *Interaction and Learning: Playgroups for parents and children (Action Research).*

Professional Appointments:

Dr. Loizou is an Associate Professor at the University of Cyprus, Nicosia, Cyprus since 2013. She has worked at other institutions including Hunter College – CUNY, New York, USA as an Assistant Professor of Early Childhood Education 2002-2003 and as an Instructor at Teachers College, NY, USA.

Publications Last 3 Years:

Loizou, E. and Avgiditou, S. (2014). The Greek-Cypriot Early Childhood Educational Reform; Introducing play as a participatory learning process and as children's right. *Early Child Development and Care* 184(12), 1884-1901.

Loizou, E. (2013). Empowering parents through an action research parenting program. *Action Research* 11(1), 73-91.

Loizou, E. (2013). Re/Conceptualization of an Early Childhood Research Laboratory Framework: Necessity, the mother of invention. *European Early Childhood Education Research Journal,* 21(4), 581-595.

Zacharia, Z., Loizou, E. and Papaevripidou, M. (2012). Is physicality an important aspect of learning through science experimentation among kindergarten students? *Early Childhood Research Quarterly,* 27(3), 447-457.

In: Humor   ISBN: 978-1-63484-787-2
Editor: Holly Phillips   © 2016 Nova Science Publishers, Inc.

Chapter 3

HUMOR, HEALTH, AND CLOSENESS TO NEIGHBORS

Chau-kiu Cheung
City University of Hong Kong, Hong Kong, China

ABSTRACT

Closeness to neighbors, including talking with and recourse to neighbors when facing difficulties, is integral to social integration. Such integration or closeness is in need of promotion or restoration in modern society. In relation to the need, one's humor and health possibly play a part, such that humor is likely to facilitate the closeness, whereas health is likely to discourage the closeness. Moreover, the likelihoods are likely to hinge on some background characteristics. Examination of all these likelihoods is necessary, considering the paucity of relevant research data. In this study, such examination engages survey data obtained from 1,170 adult in Hong Kong, China. Results show that humor reported for the previous year had a significant positive effect on current closeness to neighbors, and health in the previous month displayed a significant negative effect on the closeness. Moreover, results reveal that the negative effect of health was greater in the man and in one not living with a spouse. Results further indicate that humor in the previous year transmitted a significant positive effect on health in the previous month. Therefore, humor generated a positive direct effect and a negative indirect effect on closeness to neighbors through mediation by health. Results imply the possibility of capitalizing on humor and health concern to raise closeness to neighbors or social integration generally.

INTRODUCTION

Humor as a personal practice is vital because of presumed personal and social functions (Martin 2007). Remarkably, the functions happen in the promotion of personal health and social interaction (Fine and de Soucey 2005; Parrish and Quinn 1999). However, such functions have not been clearly demonstrable in existing research and theory. On the one hand, research has not consistently shown the contribution of humor to health through reasonable physiological processes (Martin 2001). On the other hand, theory suggests that humor expresses superiority, arrogance, and even aggression, which can undermine social integration (Martin 2007). Thus, the effects of one's humor on health and social integration are yet uncertain. The uncertainty may imply that the effects are conditional, such that some conditions moderate the effects. Possible conditions are gender, education, marital status, and other background characteristics. The moderating effects of these conditions have been uncharted. Consequently, both the main and conditional effects of humor on health and social integration, in terms of closeness to neighbors, are in need of empirical investigation. Such investigation is the aim of the present study of a random sample of Chinese adults in Hong Kong.

Humor refers to amusing one and another particularly in a tense encounter (Martin 2007). It can be an act and thus is episodic (Nezlek and Derks 2001). Even though humor can be brief and transitory, it is important because of its conspicuity and attractiveness (Martin 2007). That is, it is stimulating because it is puzzling and demanding cognitive processing (Kuiper and Borowicz-Sibenik 2005). It is also remarkable due to its incongruity, surprise, novelty, and thus creativity (Martin 2007). Moreover, humor is allegedly therapeutic and attenuating or buffering stress (Martin 2004, 2007). Such mental functioning makes humor a basis for positive psychology (Erikson and Feldstein 2007). In addition, humor tends to play a crucial role in social competence, social interaction (Fine and de Soucey 2005). Humor is also socially relevant as an indicator of social status (Crawford 2003). Research has shown the contribution of humor to social interaction (Nezlek and Derks 2001). Meanwhile, research has found the negative effects of humor on stress and fear (Abel 2002; Martin 2007).

Health refers to the person's evaluation of physical functioning or capability (Sullivan 2003). Conversely, it refers to the absence of pain or physical impairment (Svebak et al. 2004). Health is undeniably vital and subjectively viable because of the ubiquity of concern and knowledge about health (Shaw and Greenhalgh 2008). Research has shown that health is a basis leading to good life (Tomich and Helgeson 2002). Furthermore, research has indicated that health represents the resource for one to act and benefit oneself and society (Friborg et al. 2002).

Closeness to neighbors registers a crucial indicator of social integration. Such closeness or integration, as perceived by the person, is vital because of neighbors' proximity, and thus availability and accessibility (Wellman 1990). Hence, neighbors are common for social interaction (Phan et al. 2009). Neighbors are also a nucleus for development social trust (Putnam 2007). Moreover, neighbors are favorable for the exercising of social cohesion (Tolsma et al. 2007). Neighbors are furthermore the basis for developing belongingness to the neighborhood (Dekker and Bolt 2005). Research has revealed that closeness to neighbors promotes one's sense of community (Farrell et al. 2004). In addition, research has found the contribution of the closeness to commitment to and identification with the neighborhood (Hays and Kogl 2007).

THEORETICAL CONTRIBUTIONS OF HUMOR

Humor is likely to advance health through physiological processes, through physiological theory in general and psychoimmunological theory in particular. The physiological processes encompass muscular relaxation, aerobic exercising, pulmonary functioning, endocrine activation, catecholamine and cortisol secretion, and thus immunological functioning (Martin 2001, 2007). These processes are immunologically beneficial to analgesic effectiveness (Kiecolt-Glaser et al. 2002). Hence, humor has appeared to relieve pain (Martin 2007). Moreover, humor has appeared to sustain health (Boyle and Joss-Reid 2004). Particularly, coping with humor has generated a positive effect on health (Celso et al. 2003). In addition, many of the physiological processes have demonstrated their relevance to health (Ferraro and Farmer 1999). Nevertheless, much of the research has not indicated clear evidence for the salubrious effect of humor (Martin 2001).

Humor is likely to advance social integration such as closeness to neighbors, with reference to exchange theory. This theory posits that interaction that is rewarding serves to consolidate integration in the interaction (Skopek et al. 2011). Such a reward would stem from the amusing function of humor (Martin 2007). Accordingly, humor tends to be functional for maintaining rewarding communication and relationships (Fine and de Soucey 2005). In this juncture, humor has appeared to facilitate social interaction

(Nezlek and Derks 2001). Meanwhile, rewarding social interaction has exhibited its contribution to social integration (Isham et al. 2006). Particularly, interaction with neighbors has appeared to be a precursor to closeness to neighbors (Grannis 2009). Besides, humor may sustain closeness to neighbors through health. This possibility hinges on the contribution of humor to health and the contribution of health to the closeness in turn.

The contribution of health to closeness to neighbors is again explicable by exchange theory. This theory remarkably maintains rewarding exchange as a determinant of social integration (Skopek et al. 2011). In this connection, health is likely to sustain rewarding exchange as health indicates capability to uphold the relationship (Lelli 2008). Moreover, some research findings have suggested the contribution of health to social integration, such as family satisfaction, social quality, and relationship quality (Flouri and Buchanan 2002; Koromeckyj-Cox et al. 2007; van Praag and Ferrer-I-Carbonell 2004).

In contrast, health is likely to reduce closeness to neighbors with reference to need theory. The theory suggests that the need for receiving help is a determinant of social integration (Chen 2006; Volker and Flap 2007). As health tends to reduce the need for help, health is likely to diminish social integration, considering need theory (Tomich and Helgeson 2002). The possibility of the negative effect of health on closeness to neighbors thus heightens the importance of testing the hypothesis about the positive effect of health on the closeness.

What is more, humor may elevate health through social integration. Accordingly, social integration has appeared to champion one's health (Michalos et al. 2005). This salubrious effect is thus explicable by exchange theory as well. In this case, exchange theory suggests that one's humor buttresses social integration, and social integration represents a fair return to humor to boost one's health. Hence, humor may raise health through a social path, involving fair exchange and social integration.

THEORETICAL CONDITIONS FOR THE CONTRIBUTIONS

Humor is likely to contribute to health and social integration in terms of closeness to neighbors when the humor represents a socially desirable kind. Accordingly, humor involves many kinds, socially desirable and undesirable ones. Socially undesirable humor conveys aggression, arrogance, hostility, selfishness, conflict, and superiority (Cann et al. 2008; Robert and Wilbanks 2012). By contrast, socially desirable humor orchestrates affiliation, appreciation, likeability, attractiveness, tempering, and adaptation (Frewen et al. 2008; Martin et al. 2003). These socially desirable features are likely to arise from education or cultivation to meet social demands (O'Dwyer 2003). Research has therefore shown the contribution of education to social desirability (Holbrook et al. 2003). Therefore, education is likely to be a condition to render humor socially desirable. Socially desirable humor would in turn raise the exchange value of humor to facilitate health and social integration.

Marriage or living with the spouse is another condition likely to uplift social desirability (Solomon 2006). Accordingly, marriage encompasses socially desirable features such as partnership, communication, and performance satisfactory to the spouse's expectation (Elliott and Umberson 2008; Noguera et al. 2005). Therefore, research has shown that marriage is a basis for satisfaction and achievement (Yienprugsawak et al. 2010). As a socially satisfying factor, marriage is likely to enhance the socially integrative effect (Carbery and Buhrmester 1998).

Female gender is likely to be a similarly social desirable condition to enhance the socially integrative effect. The enhancement resides in the qualities of female gender in caring, tenderness, trusting, social networking, and social commitment (Carbery and Buhrmester 1998; Ferssizidis et al. 2010; Lippa 2005). These qualities has appeared to be conducive to social integration (Garcia and Herrero 2004; Isham et al. 2006).

HYPOTHESES

Major hypotheses about main effects on the individual are as follows.

1. Humor displays a positive effect on health.
2. Humor displays a positive effect on closeness to neighbors.
3. Health displays a positive effect on closeness to neighbors.

The causal order stated in the hypotheses is plausible by measuring humor in the past year, health in the recent month, and closeness to neighbors currently. That is, humor is the earliest factor and closeness to neighbors is the latest factor. Additional hypotheses maintain that education, marriage, and female gender are conditions that enhance the hypothesized main effects. That is, the hypotheses suggest that the conditions introduce positive moderating effects on the hypothesized main effects. In other words, the hypotheses envision that the hypothesized main effects are greater in the presence of the conditions.

The test of the hypotheses necessarily needs to control for possible confounding arising from background characteristics, including age, gender, marriage, living arrangement, residency, education, income, and religious affiliation. They are likely to confound the hypothesized effects due to their possible impacts on the hypothesized predictor and outcome, either closeness to neighbors or health. Age has shown a negative effect on closeness to neighbors (Swaroop and Morenoff 2006). Moreover, age has appeared to erode health (Oshio and Kobayashi 2010). The woman has tended to be lower in closeness to neighbors than has the man (Swaroop and Morenoff 2006). Moreover, the woman has appeared to be poorer in health than has the man (Borgonovi 2008). Furthermore, the woman has tended to be less humorous than has the man (Martin 2007). Education has displayed a positive effect on health (Oshio and Kobayashi 2010). Income has indicated a positive effect on closeness to neighbors (Swaroop and Morenoff 2006). Moreover, income has manifested a positive effect on health (Borgonovi 2008). The married person has appeared to be higher in closeness to neighbors than has the other (Swaroop and Morenoff 2006). Moreover, the married person has tended to be healthier than has the other (Eikemo et al. 2008). Living alone has exhibited a positive effect on closeness to neighbors (Perren et al. 2004). Moreover, living alone has exhibited a negative effect on health (Sundquist and Yang 2007). Residency has displayed a positive effect on closeness to neighbors (Bolland and McCallam 2002). Moreover, residency has tended to raise health (Islam et al. 2006).

The study happens in the context of Hong Kong, which is an amalgam of Chinese and Western influences. The Chinese heritage tends to be unfavorable to humor (Chen and Martin 2007). This heritage, remarkably stemming from Confucianism, prefers sincerity and rectitude to humor (Qian 2007). Meanwhile, the Chinese context prizes social integration, involving neighbors as well (Hu 2005). The Chinese influence is thus likely to uphold closeness to neighbors but downplay humor. This pattern seems to portray an inverse relationship between humor and closeness to neighbors. The relationship is incongruous with the hypothesized positive effect of humor on closeness to neighborhood. This incongruity thus makes the Chinese context a critical place to examine the hypothesized effect.

METHOD

Participants

The study analyzed survey data collected from 1,170 adults, based on a random sampling procedure. This procedure initially selected households randomly and then located adult members (aged 18 years or above) within the households randomly for the survey. The sampling frame was from the Census and Statistics Department of Hong Kong. Before the survey, each of the selected households received an introductory letter soliciting their participation. During the survey, trained interviewers administered the survey to ensure the acceptability of respondents' responses. After the survey, the respondents received some nominal compensation for their participation.

A weighting procedure then obtained a weighted sample in order to represent the joint distribution of age and gender in the adult population of Hong Kong. That is, oversampled cases had a lower weight, whereas under sampled cases received a greater weight. Eventually, the weighted sample yielded the following profile. The average age was 40.9 years (see Table 1). Among the sample, 63.1% were female, 61.0% were married, 57.1% were irreligious, 57.0% living with children, and 55.9% living with spouses. The average number of years in Hong Kong was 31.5 years, and that for education was 9.2 years (with 1 year for Grade 1, 2 years for Grade 2, and so on). Moreover, the average monthly income was HK$1,635 or US$210.

Measurement

Measures of humor, health, and closeness to neighbors involved multiple items using some rating scales. Eventually, the ratings generated scores on a 0-100 scale, with 0 for the lowest rating, 50 for the mid-level rating, and 100 for the highest rating. This scoring clarified the interpretation and comparison of the scores across measures (Preston and Colman 2000).

Humor in the past year was a composite of five items, such as "exploring something amusing when facing difficulties" (see Appendix). The reliability was .803.

Health in the recent month was a composite of three items, such as "health permitting getting about freely." The reliability was .641.

Closeness to neighbors currently was a composite of three items, such as "the number of neighbors regarded as close." The reliability was .617.

Table 1. Means and standard deviation (*N* = 1,170)

Predictor	Scoring	*M*	*SD*
Age	years	40.9	14.1
Living with the father	0, 100	24.4	43.0
Living with the mother	0, 100	28.9	45.3
Living with siblings	0, 100	20.3	40.3
Living with the spouse	0, 100	55.9	49.7
Living with children	0, 100	57.0	49.5
Income	ln(HK$)	7.4	0.8
Residency in Hong Kong	years	31.5	15.4
Female	0, 100	63.1	48.3
Education	years	9.2	3.6
Married	0, 100	61.0	48.8
Irreligious	0, 100	57.1	49.5
Humor	0-100	56.1	20.9
Health	0-100	74.5	21.2
Closeness to neighbors	0-100	22.5	18.3

Note. "0, 100" having a score of 0 for "no" and 100 for "yes."

Analysis

A series of linear regression analysis showed the prediction of health and closeness to neighbors, with humor, health, and background characteristics as predictors. The analysis estimated the main effects of predictors first and the interaction effects of pairs of predictors subsequently. Such pairs of predictors included those of humor and education, health and female gender, and others. Each of the pairs generated a product, by multiplying the standard scores of predictors concerned. This multiplication minimized the risk of multi-collinearity in regression analysis (Brambor et al. 2006). Essentially, the analysis only retained interaction effects that were statistically significant.

RESULTS

On average, the Hong Kong Chinese adult reported a modest level of humor during the past year (*M* = 56.1 on the 0-100 scale, see Table 1). Health, on average, was rather high in the adult during the recent month (*M* = 74.5). In contrast, closeness to neighbors was at a very low level (*M* = 22.5). This manifested a sharp deviation from Chinese tradition, which accentuates social integration.

Table 2. Standardized effects on health

Predictor	(1)	(2)
Age	-.207***	-.223***
Living with the father	.029	.025
Living with the mother	.008	.014
Living with siblings	.011	.005
Living with the spouse	.063	.065
Living with children	.052	.051
Income	.061	.058
Residency in Hong Kong	-.022	-.014
Female	-.023	-.022
Education	-.005	-.010
Married	-.019	-.008
Irreligious	-.022	-.024
Humor	.160***	.168***
Humor × Education		.095**
R^2	.088	.096

$* p < .05. ** p < .01. *** p < .001.$

Table 3. Standardized effects on closeness to neighbors

Predictor	(1)	(2)
Age	.058	.069
Living with the father	.010	.020
Living with the mother	-.130**	-.137***
Living with siblings	.011	.016
Living with the spouse	-.058	-.040
Living with children	-.018	-.024
Income	.001	-.001
Residency in Hong Kong	-.025	-.036
Female	.052	.051
Education	-.067	-.065
Married	.107	.092
Irreligious	.008	.004
Humor	.054*	.059*
Health	-.119***	-.124***
Health × Female		.093**
Health × Living with the spouse		.066*
R^2	.071	.084

$* p < .05. ** p < .01. *** p < .001.$

In predicting health in the recent month, humor displayed a significant positive main effect (β = .160, see Table 2). This effect supported Hypothesis 1. In addition, the coupling of humor and education introduced a significant positive interaction effect on health (β = .095). This effect supported the hypothesis about the conditional effect of humor, with education as a condition. Besides, age exhibited a significant negative effect on health (β = -.207). Meanwhile, education and other background characteristics did not reveal significant main effects on health.

In predicting current closeness to neighbors, humor manifested a significant positive main effect (β = .054, see Table 3). This effect supported Hypothesis 2, derived from exchange theory. In contrast, health delivered a significant negative main effect on the closeness (β = -.119). This effect contradicted Hypothesis 3, also derived from exchange theory. Instead, the negative effect lent support to the hypothesis based on need theory. That is, health tended to weaken the need for help and closeness to neighbors for receiving help eventually. In addition, two conditional effects of health were significant. One conditional effect indicated that the effect of health on closeness to neighbors was more positive in the woman than in the man (β = .093). Conversely, the effect of health was more negative in the man than in the woman. Another conditional effect revealed that the effect of health on the closeness was more positive when living with the spouse. Conversely, the effect of health on the closeness was more negative when not living with a spouse. Besides, living with the mother exhibited a significant negative effect on the closeness (β = -.130). The other background characteristics did not display significant effects on the closeness.

DISCUSSION

Results mainly demonstrate the contribution of one's humor to one's health and social integration, in terms of closeness to neighbors. Furthermore, the contribution of humor to health was greater when one's education was higher. In addition, results indicate the negative effect of health on the closeness. What is more, the effect of health was more negative when one was male or not living with a spouse. These findings are explicable with reference to some theories.

The contribution of humor to health rests on physiological theory directly and exchange theory indirectly. Accordingly, humor activates physiological processes, such as muscular relaxation and immunological functioning, which are salubrious. The main effect, nevertheless, was weak. The effect was greater when one's education was higher. The moderating effect of education might stem from the function of education to generate socially desirable and thus salubrious humor. Accordingly, social desirability in social interaction is salubrious, with respect to exchange theory. That is, humor would foster rewarding social interaction, which in turn generates rewarding social support to sustain one's health. Specifically, humor demonstrated a significant positive effect on closeness to neighborhood. Thus, humor is likely to buttress social integration, in accordance with exchange theory. That is, humor would generate a rewarding exchange to enable social integration, which in turn would safeguard health. The exchange effect would be greater when one's education was higher.

Health manifested a significant negative effect on closeness to neighbors. This effect accorded with need theory, but contradicted exchange theory. With respect to need theory, health diminishes the need for help and thus closeness to neighbors for fetching their help. The diminishment of the need was particularly greater in the man and one who did not live with a spouse. Thus, the healthy man or the healthy unmarried person was particularly less close to neighbors than was the other. It meant that the unhealthy man or unhealthy unmarried person was particularly more likely to seek help from neighbors and thus to be close with them. In other words, closeness to neighbors in the man or the unmarried person was more contingent on poor health than in others. On the one hand, this contingency reflects instrumental rationality, which is higher in the man than in the woman (Ferssizidis et al. 2010). On the other hand, the contingency reflects the sequence of recourse, such that the married person would seek help from the spouse first, whereas the unmarried person needs to seek help from neighbors (Carbery and Buhrmester 1998). Conversely, the woman has a higher orientation toward social integration than does the man (Feingold 1994). Health would strengthen the woman's capability to maintain social integration. Accordingly, health is an indicator of capability (Lelli 2008).

LIMITATIONS AND FUTURE RESEARCH

Limitations clearly happen to the single-site and single-time design of the study. On the one hand, the single site of Hong Kong poses a difficulty in generalizing the findings of the study to all adults in the world, because of the uniqueness of Hong Kong. Notably, the Chinese tradition of Hong Kong might constrain the meaning and application of humor and thus the generalizability of findings about humor. The way out of this problem would be the extension of sampling to enhance representation for adults in the world. Meanwhile, such a sample would afford the examination of contextual influence and the generality of the effects. On the other hand, the single-time study limits the certainty of causal inference in relationships among humor, health, and closeness to neighbors. Accordingly, the study cannot guarantee that humor as measured preceded health and closeness to neighbors as measured. This lack of guarantee about the temporal order would mean the indeterminacy of causal order among the factors. The solution to this problem would reside in the use of a panel design to obtain measures at different time points to ensure the temporal order. By controlling for prior measures, causal effects would be credible.

To elucidate theoretical mechanisms, future research needs to measure intermediate processes and incorporate them into mediational analysis. The theories involved in this study and in need of further investigation include physiological theory, exchange theory, and need theory. To substantiate physiological theory, physiological processes such as immunological and neurological functioning are necessary for mediational analysis in future research. For the verification of exchange theory, reward from exchange needs to be transparent for analysis. Specifically, the way that education enhances the reward merits scrutiny. To demonstrate need theory, need for help particularly that concerning health is the key for future investigation. For the investigation, how health lowers the need will be a focus. Furthermore, the moderating effects of gender and living arrangement on the need effect are indispensable for analysis.

Implications

Humor is worth promotion as a contributor to health and closeness to neighbors, at least in the Hong Kong context. Particularly, promoting humor among those with higher education would be promising for raising their health. This suggests that not all kinds of humor are equally salubrious. Instead, humor based on education would be particularly wholesome.

Closeness to neighbors would be helpful for unhealthy people, especially those who are male or not living with spouses. As such, these people would particularly benefit from the enhancement of closeness to neighbors and its helpfulness.

Besides, older people would particularly benefit more from the promotion of health and its contributor, humor. Meanwhile, those not living with their mothers would benefit from the promotion of closeness to their neighbors.

APPENDIX: ITEMS FOR MEASURING HUMOR, HEALTH, AND CLOSENESS TO NEIGHBORS

Humor, past year

- Perceiving that finding fun in the predicament would greatly reduce problems
- Talking some interesting things to ease the atmosphere when conversation becoming tense
- Smiling rather than crying when facing difficulties
- Exploring something amusing when facing difficulties
- Regarding humor as an effective means to deal with problems
- Health, recent month
- (no) Pain on the body hindering doing something necessary
- (not) needing medicines or treatments to keep body functioning to deal with daily life
- Health permitting getting about freely
- Closeness to neighbors, current
- Number of neighbors regarded as close
- Talking to neighbors when feeling blue or unwell
- Asking neighbors for help when have an economic difficulty

REFERENCES

Abel, Millicent H. 2002. "Humor, Stress, and Coping Strategies." *Humor* 15(4):365-381.
Bolland, John M., and Debra Moehle McCallum. 2002. "Neighboring and Community Mobilization in High-poverty Inner City Neighborhoods." *Urban Affairs Review* 38(1):42-69.
Borgonovi, Francesca. 2008. "Doing Well by Doing Good: The Relationships between Formal Volunteering and Self-reported Health and Happiness." *Social Science & Medicine* 66:2321-2334.

Boyle, Gregory J., and Jeanne M. Joss-Reid. 2004. "Relationship of Humour to Health: A Psychometric Investigation." *British Journal of Health Psychology* 9(1):51-66.

Brambor, Thomas, William Roberts Clark, and Matt Golder. 2006. "Understanding Interaction Models: Improving Empirical Analyses." *Political Analysis* 14:63-82.

Cann, Arnie, M. Ashley Norman, Jennifer L. Welbourne, and Lawrence G. Calhoun. 2008. "Attachment Styles, Conflict Styles and Humor Styles: Interrelationships and Associations with Relationship Satisfaction." *European Journal of Personality* 22:131-146.

Carbery, Julie, and Duane Buhrmester. 1998. "Friendship and Need Fulfillment during Three Phases of Young Adulthood." *Journal of Social & Personal Relationships* 15(3):393-409.

Celso, B.G., D.J. Ebener, and E.J. Burkhead. 2003. "Humor Coping, Health Status, and Life Satisfaction among Older Adults Residing in Assisted Living Facilities." *Aging & Mental Health* 7(6):438-445.

Chen, Chaonan. 2006. "Does the Completeness of a Household-based Convoy Matter in Intergenerational Support Exchanges?" *Social Indicators Research* 79:117-142.

Chen, Guo-hai, and Rod A. Martin. 2007. "A Comparison of Humor Styles, Coping Humor, and Mental Health between Chinese and Canadian University Students." *Humor* 20(3):215-234.

Crawford, Mary. 2003. "Gender and Humor in Social Context." *Journal of Pragmatics* 35:1413-1430.

Dekker, Karien, and Gideon Bolt. 2005. "Social Cohesion in Post-war Estates in the Netherlands: Differences between Socioeconomic and Ethnic Groups." *Urban Studies* 42(13):2447-2470.

Eikemo, Terje Andreas, Arne Matekaasa, and Kristen Ringdal. 2008. "Health and Happiness." Pp.48-64 in *Nordic Social Attitudes in a European Perspective*, edited by Heikki Ervasti, Torben Fridberg, Mikael Hjerm, and Kristen Ringdal. Cheltenham, UK: Edward Elgar.

Elliott, Sinikka, and Debra Umberson. 2008. "The Performance of Desire: Gender and Sexual Negotiation on Long-term Marriages." *Journal of Marriage & Family* 70:391-406.

Erickson, Sarah J., and Sarah W. Feldstein. 2007. "Adolescent Humor and Its Relationship to Coping, Defense Strategies, Psychological Distress, and Well-being." *Child Psychiatry & Human Development* 37:255-271.

Farrell, Susan J., Tim Aubry, and Daniel Coulombe. 2004. "Neighborhoods and Neighbors: Do They Contribute to Personal Well-being." *Journal of Community Psychology* 32(1):19-25.

Ferraro, Kenneth F., and Melissa M. Farmer. 1999. "Utility of Health Data from Social Surveys: Is There a Gold Standard for Measuring Morbidity." *American Sociological Review* 64:303-315.

Ferssizidis, Patty, Leah M. Adams, Todd B. Kashdan, Christine Plummer, Anjali Mishra, and Joseph Ciarrochi. 2010. "Motivation for and Commitment to Social Values: The Role of Age and Gender." *Motivation & Emotion* 34:354-362.

Fine, Gary Alan, and Michael de Soucey. 2005. "Joking Cultures: Humor Themes as Social Regulation in Group Life." *Humor: International Journal of Humor Research* 18(1):1-22.

Flouri, Eirini, and Ann Buchanan. 2002. "The Role of Work-related Skills and Career Role Model in Adolescent Career Maturity." *Career Development Quarterly* 51:36-43.

Frewen, Paul A., Jaylene Brinker, Rod A. Martin, and David J.A. Dozois. 2008. "Humor Styles and Personality-vulnerability to Depression." *Humor* 21(2):179-195.

Friborg, Oddgeir, Odin Hjemdal, Jan H. Rosenvinge, Monica Martinussen. 2002. "A New Rating Scale for Adult Resilience: What Are the Central Protective Resources behind Healthy Adjustment?" *International Journal of Methods in Psychiatric Research* 12(2):65-76.

Garcia, Enrique, and Juan Herrero. 2004. "Determinants of Social Integration in the Community: An Exploratory Analysis of Personal, Interpersonal and Situational Variables." *Journal of Community & Applied Social Psychology* 14:1-15.

Grannis, Rick. 2009. *From the Ground up: Translating Geography into Community through Neighbor Networks.* Princeton, NJ: Princeton University Press.

Hays, R. Allen, and Alexandra M. Kogl. 2007. "Neighborhood Attachment, Social Capital Building, and Political Participation: A Case Study of Low- and Moderate-income Residents of Waterloo, Iowa." *Journal of Urban Affairs* 29(2):181-205.

Holbrook, Allyson L., Melanie C. Green, and Jon A. Krosnick. 2003. "Telephone versus Face-to-face Interviewing of National Probability Samples with Long Questionnaires: Comparisons of Respondent Satisficing and Social Desirability Response Bias." *Public Opinion Quarterly* 67:79-125.

Hu, Yiliang. 2005. *Guanxi Community*. Beijing, China: People.

Isham, Jonathan, Jane Kolodinsky, and Garrett Kimberly. 2006. "The Effects of Volunteering for Nonprofit Organizations on Social Capital Formation: Evidence from a Statewide Survey." *Nonprofit & Voluntary Sector Quarterly* 35(3):367-383.

Kiecolt-Glaser, Janice, Lynanne McGuire, F. Robles Theodore, and Ronald Glaser. 2002. "Emotions, Morbidity and Mortality: New Perspectives from Psychoneuroimmunology." *Annual Review of Psychology* 53:83-107.

Koromeckyj-Cox, Tanya, Amy Mehraban Pienta, and Tyson H. Brown. 2007. "Women of the 1950s and the Normative Life Course: The Implications of Childlessness, Fertility timing, and Marital Status for Psychological Well-being in Late Midlife." *International Journal of Aging & Human Development* 64(4):299-330.

Kuiper, Nicholas A., and Melanie Borowicz-Sibenik. 2005. "A Good Sense of Humor Doesn't Always Help: Agency and Communion as Moderators of Psychological Well-being." *Personality & Individual Differences* 38:365-377.

Lelli, Sara. 2008. "Operationalizing Sen's Capability Approach: The Influence of the Selected Technique." Pp.310-361 in *The Capability Approach: Concepts, Measures and Applications*, edited by Flavio Comim, Mozaffar Qizilbash and Sabina Alinre. Cambridge, UK: Cambridge University Press.

Martin, Rod A. 2001. "Humor, Laughter, and Physical Health: Methodological Issues and Research Findings." *Psychological Bulletin* 127(4):504-519.

Martin, Rod A. 2004. "Sense of Humor and Physical Health: Theoretical Issues, Recent Findings and Future Direction." *Humor* 17(1/2):1-19.

Martin, Rod A. 2007. *The Psychology of Humor: An Integrative Approach*. Burlington, MA: Elsevier.

Martin, Rod A., Patricia Puhlik-Doris, Gwen Larsen, Jeanette Gray, and Kelly Weir. 2003. "Individual Differences in Uses of Humor and Their Reaction to Psychological Well-being: Development of the Humor Styles Questionnaire." *Journal of Research in Personality* 37:48-75.

Michalos, Alex C., Harvey V. Thommasen, Rua Read, Nancy Anderson, and Bruno D. Zumbo. 2005. "Determinants of Health and the Quality of Life in the Bella Coola Valley." *Social Indicators Research* 72:1-50.

Nezlek, John B., and Peter Derks. 2001. "Use of Humor as a Coping Mechanism, Psychological Adjustment, and Social Interaction." *Humor* 14(4):395-413.

Noguera, Carles Simo, Teresa Castro Martin, and Asuncion Soro Bonmati. 2005. "The Spanish Case: The Effects of the Globalization Process on the Transition to Adulthood." Pp.375-402 in *Globalization, Uncertainty and Youth in Society*, edited by Hans-Peter Blossfeld, Erik Klijzing, Melinda Mills and Karin Kurz. London: Routledge.

O'Dwyer, Shaun. 2003. "Democracy and Confucian Values." *Philosophy East & West* 53(1):39-63.

Oshio, Takashi, and Miki Kobayashi. 2010. "Income Inequality, Perceived Happiness, and Self-rated Health: Evidence from Nationwide Surveys in Japan." *Social Science & Medicine* 70:1358-1366.

Parrish, Monique M., and Patricia Quinn. 1999. "Laughing Your Way to Peace or Mind: How a Little Humor Helps Caregivers Survive." *Clinical Social Work Journal* 27(2):203-211.

Perren, Kim, Sara Arber, and Kate Davidson. 2004. "Neighboring in Later Life: The Influence of Socio-economic Resources, Gender and Household Comparison on Neighbourly Relationship." *Sociology* 38(5):965-984.

Phan, Mai B., Nadine Blumer, and Erin I. Demaiter. 2009. "Helping Hands: Neighborhood Diversity, Deprivation, and Reciprocity of Support in Non-kin Networks." *Journal of Social & Personal Relationships* 26(6-7):899-918.

Preston, Carolyn C., and Andrew M. Colman. 2000. "Optimal Number of Response Categories in Rating Scales: Reliability, Validity, Discriminating Power, and Respondent Preferences." *Acta Psychologia* 14:1-15.

Putnam, Robert D. 2007. "E Pluribus Unum: Diversity and Community In the Twenty-first Century." *Scandinavian Political Studies* 30(2):137-174.

Qian, Suoqiao. 2007. "Translating Humor into Chinese Culture." *Humor* 20(3):277-295.

Robert, Christopher, and James E. Wilbanks. 2012. "The Wheel Model of Humor: Humor Events and Affect in Organizations." *Human Relations* 65(9):1071-1099.

Shaw, Sara E., and Trisha Greenhalgh. 2008. "Best Research for What? Beat Health for Whom? A Critical Exploration of Primary Care Research Using Discourse Analysis." *Social Science & Medicine* 66:2506-2519.

Skopek, Jan, Florian Schulz, and Hans-Peter Blossfeld. 2011. "Who Contacts Whom? Educated Homophily in Online Mate Selection." *European Sociological Review* 27(2):180-195.

Solomon, Lewis D. 2006. *From Athens to America: Virtues and the Formulation of Public Policy*. Lanham, MD: Lexington.

Sundquist, Kristina, and Min Yang. 2007. "Linking Social Capital and Self-rated Health: A Multilevel Analysis of 11,775 Men and Women in Sweden." *Health & Place* 13:324-334.

Svebak, Sven, K. Gunnar Gotestam, and Eva Naper Jensen. 2004. "The Significance of Sense of Humor, Life Regard, and Stressors for Bodily Complaints among High School Students." *Humor* 17(1/2):67-83.

Swaroop, Sapna, and Jeffrey D. Morenoff. 2006. "Building Community: The Neighborhood Context of Social Organization." *Social Forces* 84(3):1665-1695.

Tomich, Patricia L., and Vicki S. Helgeson. 2002. "Five Years Later: A Cross-sectional Comparison of Breast Cancer Survivors with Healthy Women." *Psycho-Oncology* 11:154-169.

van Praag, Bernard, and Ada Ferrer-I-Carbonell. 2004. *Happiness Quantified: A Satisfaction Calculus Approach.* Oxford, UK: Oxford University Press.

Volker, Beate, and Henk Flap. 2007. "Sixteen Million Neighbors: A Multilevel Study of the Role of Neighbors in the Personal Networks of the Dutch." *Urban Affairs Review* 43(2):256-284.

Wellman, Barry. 1990. "The Place of Kinfolk in Personal Community Network." *Marriage & Family Review* 15(1/2):195-228.

Yienprugsawan, V., S. Seubsman, S. Kohamman, L.L.-Y. Lim, A.C. Sleigh, and the Thai Cohort Study Team. "2010. "Personal Wellbeing Index in a National Cohort of 87134 Thai Adults." *Social Indicators Research* 98:201-215.

In: Humor   ISBN: 978-1-63484-787-2

Editor: Holly Phillips   © 2016 Nova Science Publishers, Inc.

Chapter 4

HUMOR DETECTORS: ADOLESCENTS' THEORY OF MIND AND PERCEPTIONS OF HUMOR IN SELF AND OTHER

Sandra Leanne Bosacki

Faculty of Education, Brock University,
St. Catharines, ON, Canada

ABSTRACT

This chapter aims to bridge the gap between theory and practice in the fields of social cognition, identity, and humor within adolescence. Specifically, the purpose of this chapter is to explore connections between adolescents' theory of mind (ToM) or the ability to understand mental states in self and other, their perceptions of self-worth, and humor production and reception or detection (appreciation, understanding and comprehension) in self and others. That is, this chapter will provide a-state-of-the-science critical review of research on the development of understanding the mental world of self and other and humor in adolescence from the lens of developmental science and education. I will provide an illustrative (rather than an exhaustive) critical review of the past and present psychological research on ToM and humor experiences in adolescence. Further, this chapter will view humor production and the ability to receive and detect humor as a means of communication (visual, visual-verbal, verbal). Thus, this chapter will critically review the development of humor beliefs and perceptions, styles, understandings, creation, practices, and interests among adolescents within a personal and social-cultural context.

This chapter will explore the theory and research on the functional roles humor play in young people's personal and school lives including the cognitive, emotional, and social. Further, I will emphasize how humor perceptions and experiences influence adolescents' sense of self or identity, personal, emotional, and mental health and social adjustment and relationships (peers, teachers, family). Overall, this chapter aims to provide a critical review of research from social and psychoeducational disciplines that seek to understand the links among humor and ToM including conceptualizations, assessments, and implications of these two concepts. Such topics will include how humor plays a role in adolescents' self-concept or identity, social cognitive abilities, and school adjustment (attitudes and behaviors).

1. INTRODUCTION

Most of us can relate to emotionally uncomfortable encounters with individuals who are challenged to appreciate humor in our personal and social lives. Across the lifespan, people vary enormously in their ability to reason about others' thoughts and emotions that create a "sense of humor." The question of how we acquire this humor-mindedness or awareness, and more generally 'mind-mindedness" also known as theory of mind (ToM), has engaged researchers for almost 40 years. Early research focused on two questions with the first being the age at which children first recognize that others can have mistaken beliefs and begin to understand and express jokes and humor. The section question explored the nature of ToM and humor reception and production impairment among children with Autism Spectrum Disorders (ASD; for reviews see Hughes, 2011).

This chapter focuses on individual differences of adolescents' reasoning about identity and mental states within the context of humor, a topic that has, until recently, been overlooked. The chapter begins with an overview of research on the origins and consequences of individual differences in humor and theory of mind in the later childhood and beyond. The following section will focus on various explanations for the research findings on ToM and humor perceptions and experience within adolescence. More specifically, I will critically discuss empirical evidence that suggests cognitive (e.g., neurocognitive development), social (e.g., peers, family, social media), and cultural factors (e.g., gender, ethnicity and language, socioeconomic factors) play a role in adolescents' humor development. Finally, this chapter ends with suggestions for psychological and educational interventions and future research directions in theory and research on individual differences in humor and theory of mind.

2. HISTORICAL AND THEORETICAL BACKGROUND

2.1. Adolescence

Recently, the academic discourse of middle to late childhood and early adolescence has become increasingly complex and multivoiced (Blakemore & Mills, 2014; Del-Giudice, 2014; Siegel, 2013). The assumptions that underlie the developmental period known as emerging adolescence help shape teaching practices, curricular decisions, and social roles. However, such discourse has the potential to construct "terministic lens" that may homogenize students, and may make many of their behaviors invisible to school personnel and researchers. Such a biased approach needs to be approached with caution given the increasingly diverse and global context of human development.

Researchers suggest that in addition to biological and physical changes such as adrenarche (Del Giudice et al., 2009; Geary, 2010), students' gender stereotypic beliefs and peer relations may also help explain gender differences in academic self-belief (Bosacki, et al. 1997; Crick, 1996). However, given the complexity of emerging adolescents' social worlds, research on why girls and boys may view self-confidence and competencies in multiple contexts through different lens remains sparse (Rose & Rudolph, 2006). For example, recent findings suggest that stereotypic gender-role and cultural expectations may influence emerging adolescents' developing sense of self and their social relations. The lack of attention on sociocultural issues in developmental social cognitive science advocates the need for the exploration of sociocultural influences such as race, ethnicity, and gender (Hyde, 2014). Further in this chapter, I will discuss the role of gender and culture in humor and social cognitive development among adolescents.

2.1.1. Why Explore Social Cognitive Development and Humor in Adolescence?

For over twenty years, psychoeducational research has viewed older children and adolescents as interpretive psychologists who use a mentalistic construal of reality to make sense of their personal and social worlds

(Blakemore & Mills, 2014; Bruner, 1996). This developmental relational approach to education investigates adolescents' social understanding or social cognition, including studies that explore: "theories of mind" (Astington, 1993; Hughes, 2011), various aspects of the "self" (Harter, 1999; Marshall et al., 2014), and how these areas of social reasoning may help to explain social behavior including humor and jokes. Despite the emerging evidence that suggests a positive link exists between social-cognitive thought and social action (Hughes & Devine, 2015), few studies have examined this connection with humor beyond the school-age years (Bosacki, 2013).

Given that schools are formal organizations and have their own characteristics (values, activities, rituals, norms), the school as a culture can have an influence on all aspects of adolescents' development. Although school provides a data-rich context in which to explore how adolescents' make sense out of their social and personal worlds, little is known about the role that social-cognitive processes play in self-development and social relations within the school context (Eccles & Roeser, 2003; Hughes, 2011). As Bruner (1996) states, viewed from a psychological-cultural lens, schools have the potential to create a climate that can either promote or impede self-expression, cognitive and emotional growth, and self-compassion.

Similarly, relational, developmental systems approach to social understanding focuses on emerging adolescents' ability to recognize themselves and other people as psychological beings. This approach draws on social-cognitive and epistemological theories and research (Selman, 1980; Tomasello, 2014), and may help to make sense of the psycho-social studies that show a significant drop in self-worth and an increase in reflection and self-conscious emotions during the transition to adolescence Although school provides a data-rich context in which to explore how adolescents' make sense out of their social and personal worlds, (Harter, 1985). There is also substantial evidence that shows a decline in academic motivation, school attachment and academic achievement across the emerging adolescence years (Eccles & Roeser, 2003; Simmons & Blyth, 1987). Such developments may help to shape how adolescents create their personal worlds, and how they choose to relate to others. That is to say, schools have an important impact on how adolescents choose to "voice" or express their thoughts and feelings.

Given the complexities surrounding the emerging adolescent experience, the adolescent personal fable has often been discussed in negative terms because of its potentially self-harmful consequences. That is, some risk-taking older children and adolescents may believe that they are immune to social and emotional problems experienced by others (Blakemore & Mills, 2014; Finy et al., 2014; Elkind, 1967). Such risk-takers may tend to disregard natural physical limitations, sometimes even the permanence of death. Moreover, such beliefs of infallibility may lead to the engagement of risk-taking behaviors (e.g., driving while inebriated or texting, engagement in extreme risk sports).

The personal fable, however, may also have protective value against suicidal, self-harming, and depressive behavior. For example, Cole (1989) found that adolescents who endorsed life-affirming values and optimistic views of the future, and were less likely to resort to suicidal thoughts or behavior. Cole hypothesized that adolescents who have a strong sense of their own invulnerability, and whom do not view themselves as possible targets for silencing, nor feel the need to silence their own voices, will likely see themselves as capable of effectively coping with life challenges. Thus, Cole supports the idea that aspects of the adolescent personal fable may act as a buffer against suicidal thoughts and harmful behavior – to self and other (Larson, 2011).

In contrast, impulsivity that may be sometimes fueled by the belief of invincibility and coupled with a failure to recognize one's own limitations, has the potential to lead young people to feel alienated or disconnected from their family members and friends. Such impulsive tendencies may also lead youth to develop self-critical, punitive, and cruel thoughts and perhaps attempt self-harmful behaviors such as suicide (Nock et al., 2009). Seligman (2011) among others suggest that the psychobiological changes that characterize late childhood and early adolescence may leave some young people at risk. For example, the transition to adolescence may include a heightened sense of self-consciousness, fluctuating hormonal levels, an incoherent, unstable sense of self, and a degree of impulsivity. Such factors may create the foundation for the development of future social and emotional challenges such as conduct and impulse challenges (Del Giudice et al., 2009), and anxiety and internalizing or self-harm tendencies (Brinthaupt et al., 2009). The developmental characteristics of emerging adolescence may place particular youth at a heightened risk for an inappropriate response to stress under the most optimal or ideal circumstances. (Larson, 2011; Rose, 2014; Siegel, 2013). Even a relatively minor perceived loss or rejection or disappointment in oneself has the potential to trigger self-destructive urges and thoughts, which can lead to self-silencing, self-alienation and self-harm (Callan et al., 2014).

Later childhood and early adolescence is also a crucial time when many youth establish a degree of autonomy from their family and take significant steps in personal identity formation. At the same time, peer relationships become increasingly important during the late childhood and early adolescent years. Family and peers may have positive and negative consequences for a young person's private speech and experiences of social silences. In the cases where emerging adolescents do not feel comfortable to voice their own opinions, they may distance themselves from their friends and families.

Also, given most developed countries support a relatively age-stratified society, emerging adolescents and their peers may interact within a social milieu that may lack support (Blakemore & Mills, 2014; Robbins, 1998). Thus, adolescents may feel that their personal voice is silenced and not valued by their family or peers, which in turn may lead to greater self-silencing, and consequent social and emotional challenges such as negative affect, anxiety, and depression, self-harming behavior, or aggressive and impulsive behaviors among others (Del Giudice, 2014).

2.2. Theory of Mind

Early research on the development and variability in children's understanding of mind began when Dunn and colleagues (1991) argued that this variability might contribute to later individual differences in young people's emotional and social development. Based on Dunn and colleagues' work, methodological advances have driven changes in our understanding of developmental and individual differences in ToM. Recent advances of ToM research focus on larger and more diverse samples across time, and the construction of task batteries to produce continuous measures sensitive to variation in ToM performance. Such task batteries may help to document individual differences in success rates on tests of ToM in childhood to emerging adolescents (Hughes & Devine, 2015). This recent developmental approach to ToM challenges the traditional view that the development of theory of mind is an all-or-nothing matter.

Echoing the findings from research on preschoolers, several studies have documented cross-sectional associations in school-age children and adolescents between individual differences in ToM and executive function performance (Lagatutta et al., 2014), and measures of language ability (Devine & Hughes, 2013). Likewise, following a developmental, relational approach, another study that explored the variation in parents' use of terms referring to cognitive states (e.g., think, know) predicted individual differences in children's ToM at ages 6 and 10 (Devine & Hughes, 2013). Findings from preschool interventions have stimulated school-based group interventions in which discussions of mental states produced significant improvements in the mental-state reasoning of Italian 9-year-olds (Leece et al., 2014).

As results from educational and intervention ToM studies show, the approach to adolescence includes widened social circles– especially within the school context. For example, the transition from primary to secondary school expands young people's social horizons, although at the same time the boundaries between self and other may become more porous as young people enter adolescence. That is, the young person's sense of self or well-being may be more vulnerable to outside influences such as peer relations which in turn may affect their ToM reasoning. In particular, peer acceptance in middle childhood was found to longitudinally predict associations with later understanding of ToM as measured by faux pas stories (Banerjee et al., 2011). Given the reciprocal connections between social environments and children's variation in theory of mind, the mixed findings from studies of twins also suggest a developmental shift, with heritability estimates gradually decreasing across the first decade of life (Hughes & Devine, 2015).

Although Theory of Mind (ToM) development or the ability to understand thoughts and emotions in self and other is an active area of research (Dunn, 2008), empirical evidence gleaned from the later childhood regarding the relations between social understanding and perceptions of perceived self-worth remains sparse (Hughes, 2011). In addition, there remains a dearth of longitudinal studies that explore if reasoning about self (intrapersonal) and other (interpersonal) are reciprocal and interdependent, or remain isolated and independent from one another (Lucariello, 2005) during the transition from childhood to adolescence. To address this gap in the research, the following section will explore connections among adolescents' theory of mind, perceptions of self-worth, and perceptions of humor in self and others.

Children's Understanding of Mind and Emotion. The development of the ability to represent and reason from second-order beliefs (two or more mental states) has received relatively little attention in the literature particularly during the emerging adolescence (e.g., 8 – 12 years) (Bosacki, 2015; Hughes, 2011). The importance of second-order or interpretive reasoning has been shown in relation to children's ability to understand speech acts such as lies, jokes, sarcasm, and irony (Filoppova & Astington, 2008, 2010; Leekam, 1993), and in their ability to understand self-representational display rules (Banerjee & Yuill, 1999; Banerjee & Watling, 2007). Given that advanced or higher order social reasoning may also help adolescents understand the ambiguous nature of personal and social silences (Bosacki, 2015), some researchers suggest such advanced reasoning is also fundamental to adolescents' understanding of self-conscious or social moral emotions (e.g., embarrassed, proud), their sense of self and other persons, and social interactions (Hughes, 2011).

To support this developmental view of social cognition, recent evidence suggests that emotion understanding continues to develop during middle childhood to late childhood (approximately during the ages 8-12 years), particularly regarding the understanding of complex and ambiguous emotions (Pons, et al., 2003, 2004; Yuill & Coutlas, 2007). In contrast to the simple or basic emotions (e.g., happy, sad), to understand complex or socio-moral emotions (e.g., pride, embarrassment), children must hold in mind two separate pieces of information: other people's and societal norms (Saarni, 1999). That is, adolescents must imagine what others think of their behavior and self-evaluate their behaviour against internalized behavioral standards. Although complex emotion understanding hinges on cognitive abilities such as second-order socio-moral reasoning and self-evaluation, to date, no studies have investigated the links between these concepts during the transition from childhood to adolescence.

Although ToM and self-perceptions would appear to be foundational to child's educational experiences (Bruner, 2006), few researchers have studied the relations between ToM understanding, self-perceptions, and school experiences beyond the age of 8 or 9 either within their family or school context (Bosacki, 2008). Similar to the rich family context, the school classroom provides children with a valuable opportunity to learn social and emotional messages regarding interactions and others' mental states. Regarding academic competence and school success, associations have been found between ToM and the production of stories and general language ability (Hughes, 2011). Theory of mind understanding has also been claimed to facilitate children's ability to self-monitor and regulate their cognitive process and engage in reflexive thinking (Lagattuta & Wellman, 2002).

2.3. Humor

2.3.1. Definitions and Developmental Research on Humor: Humor Detectives in Training?

Humor has been studied within a diverse array of fields and disciplines, such as philosophy, psychology, sociology, anthropology, and linguistics (Dynel, 2009). This multidisciplinary groundwork has produced a number of theories, definitions, and taxonomies. For example, Berger (2013) identified up to 45 techniques of humor that include absurdity, exaggeration, literalness, repetition, and unmasking, among others. Several of these techniques have a reverse form (e.g., exaggeration/understatement), and could be combined (Martin 2007; Berger, 2013), the variety of forms and discursive functions of humor may also increase. Given such a complex and broad topic, the operational definition of humor for this chapter is "any communicative instance which is perceived as humorous" (Martineau, 1974, p.114), or that elicits amusement, laughter, or, more broadly, a "social smile" (Ziv, 2010, p. 11). Specifically, the interactional and conversational dimensions of the humor process can be viewed as a discursive tool to achieve situated social goals. (Tannen, 1994).

Humor processing may hold special functions during the relationally complex time of adolescence. For example, the expression and understanding of humor such as "getting it," and laughing at it, has the potential to reassure the sender and the receiver of the humorous message, as they co-construct shared ground for communication. That is, the collective use of humor in socially complex and ambiguous environments such as the teenagers' social world may be interpreted as a collaborative process that has the potential to perpetuate humor. This collaborative act of humor may also involve a series of messages (verbal and nonverbal such as gestures) that create a combination of spontaneous joking and confirmatory laughter (Hübler & Bell, 2003). However, some research suggests that humor and laughter may not necessarily be codependent. That is, the study of context-specific and social uses of humor or what we accomplish with humor rather than the form, can help us to better understand its functions, besides and beyond the elicitation of smiling, laughter, or amusement.

Research shows that humor can help to foster the development and maintenance of social relationships, ease the sense of uncertainty that may arise in human interactions, and facilitate social communication (Hübler & Bell, 2003). As youth position themselves within the group through conversational peer discourse, the ability to successfully produce humor in a community is often connected to peer recognition and social desirability (Martin, 1998; Pennington & Hall, 2014). An appropriate use of humor can increase players' satisfaction and trust as they exchange social skill knowledge, form shared understandings, and engage in a discursive exploration of affinity (Graham, 1995; Kurtzberg et al., 2009). Such uses may help to narrow social distances between 'players' within the 'game of humor' (Brown & Levinson, 1978). Within a learning community of adolescents, humor has the potential to alleviate tensions and conflicts (Lefcourt, 2001), increase emotional intimacy, and strengthen interpersonal bonds (Martineau, 1972). Humor may also contribute to group well-being, and an overall shared atmosphere or emotional climate of enjoyment, psychological safety, and pleasure (Ziv, 2010).

According to Yuill (2009), children in the early years of schooling as well as young adolescents show important changes in their understanding of the relation between text and meaning. For example, preschoolers and preteens show an increasing ability to discriminate between verbatim and paraphrase (Lee, Torrance & Olson, 2001), the explicit recognition of interpretive ambiguity (Bonitatibus & Beal, 1996) and the judgement of spoken message adequacy (e.g., Robinson & Robinson, 1983). Olson (1996) argued that the acquisition of literacy brings the understanding that the wording of a text is fixed, but its meaning is subject to interpretation. The interpretive nature of text is particularly salient in the rather specific case of ambiguity derives from lexical or structural properties of language, where there are two quite different interpretations of a text are plausible. For example, homonyms and jokes are often based on linguistic ambiguity and multiple meanings.

Verbal jokes belong to a genre of language in which multiple interpretations are the explicit focus: to 'get' a joke is to appreciate how a particular context misleads us into the wrong interpretation of an ambiguous text. Consider the following joke: 'Why did the tomato blush – because it saw the salad dressing.' The term 'salad dressing' could be considered as either a noun phrase, – or a noun (salad) and verb (dressing). Thus, the humor effect can only be achieved through the interpretation of the syntax as reading 'salad' as a noun, and 'dressing' as a verb.

Children may understand the basic possibility of lexical and structural ambiguity at a relatively early age, but past studies show individual differences over a wide age range in ambiguity understanding. For example, even in the basic understanding that one word can have different meanings, there is an early conceptual recognition of homonymy at the age of 4 (Doherty, 2000), but many children show poor performance, even up to early adolescence or around the age of 10 or 11, in the selection of referents for pseudohomonyms (Doherty, 2004). Similarly, most neurotypical children from the age of around 7 or 8 show competence in understanding at least some types of verbal humor (Yuill, 2009), but there are wide individual differences in 7- to 10-year-olds in the ability to recall and explain such jokes (Bosacki, 2013).

These individual differences in understanding structural ambiguity in language may stem from two general types of process, both of which require further investigation. First, some children may have difficulties with the automatic aspects of processing that affect their interpretation of ambiguous text. For example, Gernsbacher (1990) suggested that activation of irrelevant meanings of ambiguous words competes with the correct interpretation, and less-skilled readers may fail to suppress such irrelevant meanings, or to enhance activation of relevant meanings. Second, Long, Seely and Oppy (1999) suggested that more controllable and strategic processes may affect the selection of appropriate meaning in readers with varied abilities, which would be particularly evident in tasks that have metacognitive demands (e.g., judgments of meaning rather than lexical decision). Building on previous research on understanding of ambiguity at the strategic level in children reading comprehension (Yuill, 2009), how can researchers apply these findings to explore how adolescents make sense of social and linguistic ambiguity and humor in their social context of the classroom? In addition, as I explore in the next section, how does this understanding of linguistic ambiguity relate to emerging adolescents' understanding of humor in self and others, and what does this means for the adolescent's mental and social worlds?

2.3.2. Ambiguity and Humor

Given Empson's (1947) claim that jokes have a moral component and depend on an ambiguity with both cases having contradictory meanings (e.g., scale of noble/naughty/intellectual/instinctual, p. 246), research on children's understanding of humor, cynicism, irony, and sarcasm may to uncover how adolescents make sense of social and personal ambiguity within the classroom (Filoppova & Astington, 2008; Mills & Keil, 2005; Recchia, Howe, Ross, & Alexander, 2010).

By the age of 6 to 7 years, children begin to understand the concept of double meanings which allows them to start appreciating jokes and riddles. Given that research suggests that development of cognition and humor are inextricably connected (McGhee, 1984), most of the work on humor focused on children's perception of humorous incongruities (Bariaud, 1989; McGhee; Schultz, 1976), and were conducted in experimental settings with graphic stimuli materials and smiling and laughter as indicators of humor.

In relation to understanding sarcasm and irony, humor is an exclusive and complicated human phenomenon, which depends on many factors (McGhee, 1977; McGhee & Goldstein, 1983; Paulos, 1980, Semrud-Clikeman & Glass, 2010). Thus, although most researchers agree that cognitive development is the basic element of the ability to appreciate and understand humor, the role of humor in social emotional and moral development are less explored (Bergen, 2008; Lyons & Fitzgerald, 2004; McGhee, 1984).

Drawing on research findings of children' understanding interpretive ambiguity within text and conversations (Beal & Bonitivus, 1996; Torrance & Olson, 1991), research on metaphor, irony, sarcasm, lying, and humor reveal that children in middle childhood and early adolescence are more likely to understand the meaning of ambiguous statements based on the intonation of the speaker. For example, studies on sarcasm found that if children heard an ambiguous statement with a negative intonation, they would interpret the statement as sarcastic (Capelli, et al., 1990).

2.3.3. School as a Humor Rich Context

Given the complex school context of the adolescent, the development of the ability to understand and produce jokes in childhood and adolescence, has been examined by many (Bernstein, 1986; Bariaud, 1988; Cameron, et al., 2001; Radomska, 2007). To understand and create humor, irony, and generally ambiguous statements, learners need to go beyond literal meaning and develop the ability to represent mental states. Given this ability to represent physical events in the mind, humor perception and production is a very valuable way to research how young people understand mental states within the classroom (Filippova & Astington, 2008). Furthermore, humor comprehension may reflect a child's ability to differentiate between "what you said and what you really meant and how you feel." Thus, the perception that other people act intentionally plays a critical role in ToM, and helps young people to understand the meanings behind people's actions (with or without humor) within the school setting. This ability to understand the mental world of others helps young people to decipher ambiguous social and humorous events in the classroom among their peers and teachers as described in sections below.

3. RESEARCH ON HUMOR AND THEORY OF MIND IN ADOLESCENCE

3.1. Personal

3.1.1. ToM, Humor, and Self-Concept

ToM and Humor. Although the ability to create and understand jokes may help us to learn how children and adolescents develop an understanding of mental states in others in ambiguous situations, the processes of creating and understanding jokes are usually researched separately. Examples of past research involve the creation or production aspect of humor such as using humor as a coping skill to deal with social and emotional situations in one's life (Fuhr et al., 2015). Alternatively, past studies have explored the idea that humor perception could be interpreted as a weathervane for emerging psycholinguistic, social and cognitive abilities such as understanding intentionality, persuasion, and symbolism (Martin, 2007).

To explore the relation between the two processes of humor production and perception and how they relate to ToM, Kielar-Turska and Bialecka- Pikul (2009) studied 5- to 9-year-old Polish children's ability to generate and understand visual jokes as an expression of ToM. Kielar-Turska and Bialecka-Pikul asked children to draw a funny picture and then justify what made it funny, as well as to produce a funny story. Two months later children were presented with selected drawings and they were asked to judge whether or not the drawing was funny. Overall, findings suggest that children's ability to understand the artist's intention increased with age, suggesting that the relation between a more complex, interpretive ToM and the ability to understand jokes increased with age. Moreover, findings suggested that children were more likely to find a drawing funny if their friend found it to be funny, and thus supports Zygulski's (1976) claim that the community of laughter as reflected in family and peer environments may influence a child's perceptions of humor (Żygulski, 1976).

Given that cultural psychologists view culture and mind as inseparable, and argue that there are no common rules pertaining to how the mind works (Bruner, 1996; Tomasello, 1999; Johnson & Mervis, 1997; Lillard, 1997; Wellman et al., 2006; Xeromeritou, 2004), future researchers should continue to explore how culture and mind influence humor reception and production in youth as humor plays a large role in young people's social interactions and identity. For example, Kielar-Turska and Bialecka-Pikul (2009) explored humor understanding as represented by children's understanding of funny drawings in a variety of countries and compare findings. Thus, what is found to be humorous in one culture may not be viewed as such in another culture. Martin (2007) maintains that humor and laughter are universal in all cultures, but that cultural approaches may vary.

However, there has been little cross-cultural comparison of humor as it relates to social cognitive development. For example, Americans were found to have a higher sense of humor in the area of creativity than their Spanish counterparts (Thorson, Valero, & Carbelo Baquero, 2006). Chinese university students, as compared to Canadian norms, were reported to have significantly lower scores on humor styles and coping humor (Chen & Martin, 2007). In Western cultures, especially American culture, humor plays a main role in creativity and personality, unlike in the Chinese culture humor where it plays the least important role (Yue, 2008).

Given these mixed results, future research needs to continue to explore the role culture, age, and gender play in children's and adolescents' understanding of ambiguous contexts such as humor (McNamara, 2004). Such past research findings suggest that the ability to understand humor within ambiguous situations may lead to positive learning experiences and help children to develop a sense of resilience, later in this chapter I will outline strategies to incorporate humor into holistic, inclusive educational programs for adolescents.

Researchers need to continue to explore children's understanding of complex and ambiguous situations within the context of peer relations, especially during early and middle adolescence. That is, during social situations, teenagers may use subtleties of language through the use of irony, sarcasm, or teasing to sometimes mask negative and hurtful judgemental statements about their peers. Given the linguistic and emotional ambiguities of such statements –competent youth who understand these double meanings may be more sensitive to such emotional ambiguity in that they are interpreted as hurtful statements which may possibly may have a negative and damaging influence on their sense of self.

Given that most adolescents co-construct a sense of self or possible selves (Markus & Kitayma, 1994; Markus & Wurf, 1987), and that "every relationship implies definition of self by other and other by self" (Laing, 1969, p. 86), they may be cautious or hesitant to communicate their authentic self with feeling and thoughts. A person's identity or identities cannot be completely abstracted from her/his interactions with others. That is, an young person's identity-for-herself, the identity others ascribe to her; the identities she attributes to them; the identities she thinks her friends and family attribute all influence what she thinks her friends think, and how she thinks that they think about her. Such complex self-reflective thought has implications for humor and how it is understood especially among peer relations as friendships play an important role among young people.

During adolescence as the self continues to develop, the definition of self becomes a challenge as it becomes increasingly complex to imagine one's true self – given the multiple definitions of the self. In addition to Markus and Wurf's (1985) notion of dynamic and changing selves, Harter's (1999) explores multiple selves such as social, academic, athletic, behavioral conduct, physical appearance and also a general sense of well-being and in addition to the task of juggling these multiples selves, adolescents also have the task of negotiating between their 'real' or 'ideal' self - and how do they relate to one another. According to Kahneman (2003), we have our self that we experience, and our self that we remember, as our experienced selves are what we experience during life events such as a social interaction including which may be associated with particular thoughts and emotions. In addition, we have our remembered selves that takes into account the cognitive markers of the event and how this influences our sense of personal well-being regarding our thoughts and emotions.

As Kahneman (2003) asserts, these selves may not always correlate with each other. That is, the individual will need to negotiate these selves within the personal landscape. This task of negotiating the various selves further adds to the complex emotional landscape of the adolescent, particularly during the school context, with implications for our emotional well-being including our feelings of happiness (Harris, 2010). The multiple selves also have implications for how adolescents understand and produce humor within themselves, as well as their interactions with others. In the following sections, I will discuss past research in humor with the personal and social worlds of the adolescent (Harris, 2010).

ToM, Self-Perceptions, and Humor. Humor is an important component of social interaction, generating laughter, amusement, exhilaration, mirth and other positive emotions (Martin, 2007; Ruch, 2007). Interestingly, the relation between humor perception or production and emotion among youth has yet to be studied within the context of Theory of Mind (the ability to ascribe mental states to other people). The few studies that exist suggest research on connections between adults' Theory of Mind and perceptions of humor found positive links between adults' understanding of mental states in self and other and their ability to understand concepts of humor and what makes a statement or comic strip 'funny.' or humorous (Samson et al., 2012, in-press). More recently, Bosacki (2013) found positive relations between 8 year old Canadian children's ToM score and their ability to perceive humor in ambiguous social stories 2 years later at 10 years of age.

Given the lack of research on children and adolescents' ToM and perceptions of self and humor, research needs to continue to investigate the individual differences in, and the relations among ToM, self-perceptions, and perceptions of humor over time. For example, a recent study found that Canadian children's understanding of humor in self and other was partially related to their ToM and self-concept over time. In particular, Bosacki (2013) found that between the ages of 8 years and 10 years children's understanding of humor in self and others developed in complexity, and related to children's self-perceptions as well as their ToM ability.

Humor as Way of Emotional Coping – Case Study of Gelotophia and Shyness. Gelotophobes particularly fear being laughed at and appearing ridiculous to their social partners. They experience humor as aversive and as a means to put them down (Platt & Forabosco 2012 for an overview). Except for two studies (Proyer, Neukom et al., 2012; Proyer & Neukom 2013) there are few studies on gelotophobia in children and adolescents (Führ, 2010; Proyer et al., 2013). However, there are many open questions on gelotophobia in childhood and adolescence including its causes and consequences. There is evidence that children use humor as a coping mechanism (Masten, 1986), and this ability may contribute positively to avoiding gelotophobia and its detrimental effects. Since most of the studies in the field were conducted with adults, Fuhr et al., (2015) studied gelotophobia or the fear of being laughed at in 1,322 Danish adolescents aged 11 to 16.

More specifically, Fuhr et al., (2015) studied coping humor in three different respects (1) to overcome stress and uncertainty, (2) in relation to aggression and sexuality, and (3) to boost one's mood or to cheer oneself up. Results showed that the fear of being laughed at existed independently from the use of humor as a coping strategy. Fuhr et al., suggested that interventions need to target the positive use of laughter and humor as such programs may help to increase the well-being of adolescents with high levels of the fear of being laughed at. In single item ratings higher levels of gelotophobia were associated with greater self-ascribed loneliness, lower perceived attractiveness, lower self-acceptance, and rather negative life expectancies. In addition to teaching youth to learn how to use humor as a coping mechanism, Fuhr et al., also suggested that educational programs need to help teach youth to learn how to read emotions in general within themselves and others, particularly with a focus on positive emotions.

Humor can also be viewed as a way of coping or managing one's emotions during times of stress such as social situations (Masten, 2008). For example, Markovic and Bowker (2015) recently explored the role of humor in anxious-withdrawn (also referred to as shy or anxious-solitary) young adolescents' peer relations and perceived identities. Humor may be perceived as a valued characteristic among young adolescents as a means to popularity or peer acceptance. More specifically, Markovic and Bowker found that although humor was perceived by peers to be a valued characteristic among their anxious-withdrawn peers, for boys only, humor was found to serve as a protective factor. In other words, anxious-withdrawn males perceived as funny by their peers were also perceived as more popular. Perhaps for those boys who their peers considered them to be funny and athletic, humor may have served as a buffer against the emotional harm and decrease in popularity that may emerge from overt victimization. Such results support past research that shows that other socially vulnerable groups of youth (e.g., aggressive, rejected, etc.) who are perceived to be funny, may also be perceived as socially competent by their peer group (Knack et al., 2012).

In contrast, Markovic and Bowker (2015) failed to find that displays of humor protected anxious-withdrawn girls against overt victimization or enhanced their popularity. Given that self-defeating humor commonly reflects low self-esteem (Hampes, 2006; Klein & Kupier, 2006), young adolescents may recognize that the self-disparaging jokes of anxious-withdrawn girls stem from negative talk and feelings about the self. Thus, despite being entertained and, even enjoying the company of anxious withdrawn girls, peers may continue to perceive these girls as socially inferior and thus easy targets for overt victimization.

Although some youth who are perceived to be funny, nice, good-looking, and athletic by their peers may also be perceived as socially competent (Lease et al., 2002), future research should examine the social-cognitive mechanisms of ToM that may enable peers to interpret these qualities when they are coupled with anxious-withdrawn behaviors. However, to date, Markovits and Bowker's (2015) is the first study to show how the protective component of humor may have the potential to generalize to anxious-withdrawn young adolescent boys.

It has been found that shy adolescent and adult males who display humor tend to use aggressive humor such as jokes that involve hostility, sarcasm, and demeaning or negative comments (Hampes, 2006). Further research is needed on the role of humor as a buffer or protective factor against harmful teasing and bullying in adolescents across all gender orientations including transgendered youth (Proyr, et al., 2013). Thus, past research suggests that humor is a common and highly effective coping strategy used to help youth deal with stressful situations during adolescence (Erickson & Feldstein, 2007; Fuhr et al., 2015; Geisler & Weber, 2010). Researchers need to further investigate how humor may help to marginalize youth to cope more adaptively with stress and their fears and anxieties.

3.2. Social Relations

3.2.2. ToM and Humor in Friendships

As discussed earlier, humor can help to serve as a psychological and emotional coping strategy to help a person deal with negative emotions. In addition, humor can also be used to serve as a communication tool to develop friendships and strengthen social and psychological bonds with others (Marone, 2015). Given the importance of peer relations within adolescence, humor plays an important social functions within adolescence. For example, humor has the potential to help strengthen emotional bonds among friends, and may also serve as a mechanism to cope with bullying and aggressive behaviours, and related negative emotions such as anxiety and depression (Marone, 2015).

Past studies with younger children highlight the importance of humor as a social and communicative competence, and as a life-attitude to help one cope with human relationships and life experiences (Fuhr, 2002). More specifically, Fuhr showed that a group of Danish adolescents reported evidence of having humor as an attitude toward life. That is, Fuhr showed that adolescents who reported a high humor coping style reported to be less lonely and had a positive view of their personality. Furthermore, adolescents who reported a well-developed sense of humor showed greater self-confidence, were more popular, and found it easier to create positive friendships and social situations. Combined with similar studies with adults, the majority of research on the social role of humor shows that the ability to use humor in daily life situations appears to be a strong predictor for wellbeing and happiness.

Overall, the majority of empirical evidence on adults and children indicates that those individuals with a well-developed sense of humor are more likely to show a greater self-confidence, are more popular, less lonely and find it easier to establish positive relations and friendship with their peers (Marone, 2015). Furthermore, the ability to use humor in various daily life situations appears to be a strong predictor for happiness and wellbeing.

Given the role language plays in social interactions and the formation of relationships, youth who experience cognitive and communication impairments may have difficulty understanding a speaker's goals in a conversation and how an utterance serves those goals. Impairment in these areas could leave an adolescent unable to appreciate fully, for example, humor, as well as deception, sarcasm, and irony which are common and important features of natural conversation within school contexts. As I discussed earlier in the chapter, a current organizational framework for analysing these aspects of communication is termed Theory of Mind (ToM) or the ability to use other people's beliefs to understand or predict behaviour.

As I explain further on in the chapter, intervention programs that include strategies to help young people learn how to read facial expressions and their corresponding emotions may help them form caring and supportive friendships and thus feel less isolated and lonely (Lundgren & Brownell, 2015). ToM and humor may also be relevant to other cognitive tasks, such as the ability to distinguish accidental from intentional harm and intentional from unintentional violation of social norms. The exciting possibility is that training ToM may affect performance in selected social cognitive domains, and thereby increase the usefulness of intervention (Cushman, 2008). Future suggestions for further classroom interventions to promote ToM and humor are discussed further on in this chapter.

4. EXPLANATIONS – HOW DO WE EXPLAIN HUMOR STYLES AND BEHAVIORS?

Past research suggests that the degree to which someone experiences amusement evoked by a joke or funny event may depend on several factors. For example, different people may perceive humorous stimuli differently, as their interpretations depend on a variety of personality characteristic, and social cognitive styles. Examples include 1) experience seeking (Forabosco & Ruch, 1994; Ruch & Hehl, 2007), 2) sense of humor (e.g., Martin et al., 2003; see also Martin, 2007), 3) emotional responsiveness (Herzog & Anderson, 2000), or 4) temperamental mood states such as cheerfulness, seriousness, and a general bad mood (Ruch, Köhler, & van Thriel, 1997). In addition, cognitive and linguistic skills such as verbal fluency, cognitive flexibility, (Shammi & Stuss, 2003), and Theory of Mind may influence humor processing (Samson & Hegenloh, 2010).

The reviewed findings suggest that complex connections exist among adolescents' ToM, humor perceptions and self-perceptions. Such findings support previous research (Bosacki, 2008; Hughes, 2011), and theorists' claims that self-concept and humor understanding and experiences may play significant roles in young people's ToM understanding (Bruner, 1996; Gergen, 2001).

How can researchers explain a connection between humor and identity? Consider for example the following finding that 8 year old children's perceptions of the physical self or physical appearance were negatively related to their humor understanding 2 years later (Bosacki, 2013), perhaps this negative relation supports the claim that the self-concept is a multidimensional and dynamic process that contains various dimensions that may or may not be related to each other (Harter, 1999). As social cognitive researchers claim (Bussey & Bandura, 2004), we need to know which self-regulatory functions play roles in humor processing and production, and how this differs according to gender, ethnicity, and socioeconomic status. Thus, the reviewed findings add to the growing body of empirical evidence regarding individual differences and longitudinal relations in young people's ToM, humor perceptions, and self-concept.

What are the social and cultural explanations of findings that show humor perception and production differ according to one's cultural backgrounds? That is, how can such findings be explained within a social, historical, and cultural framework in terms of using humor as a social or cultural glue to emotionally bond others together? Based on past research (Bosacki, 2013), compared to males, perhaps some females who are more likely to understand mental states in others are also more capable of perceiving humor in self and others in the middle childhood and early adolescent years. Given that gender is a culture (Maccoby, 1998), such gender-related differences may be in part due to societal cultural messages that encourage females to remain positive and maintain a sense of humor to please others (Tannen, 1994; Layard & Dunn, 2009; Walker, 2005). As outlined in the next section, these findings provide implications for future research that explores how adolescents' higher ToM abilities may lead them to imagine both the positive and negative interior worlds of others (Hughes, 2011).

From a psychocultural and social cognitive perspective, (Bussey & Bandura, 2004; Bronfenbrenner, 1977; Maccoby, 1998), the present findings can be explained in terms of the interplay among self-perceptions, humor processing, stereotypic societal gender-role expectations and Theory of Mind. For example, why did Bosacki (2013) find that 8-year-old children who claimed to be happy with their physical appearance were more likely to have self-perceived humor and lower Theory of Mind scores? Perhaps some children at 8 and 9 years old who were dissatisfied with their physical appearances may also have been more likely to refer to humor in their self-descriptions as a coping strategy to deal with their negative self-feelings two years later as the approached 10-11 years (Klein & Kupier, 2006). This result may suggest that pre-teen children who are more likely to understand the complex mental world of others are also more likely to view their physical sense of selves negatively as they could imagine their friends having negative judgements about them. Alternatively, children who are less likely to understand that others have mental lives, may be more likely to report being happy with their physical appearance as they are either unable, or uninterested in imagining what their peers are thinking of them.

Past research studies that show females score higher than male on humor reception and production may reflect stereotypic societal gender-role expectations which place a greater value on emotional and humor competence among women as compared to men (Bosacki, 2013). Perhaps girls learn in school that understanding humor in self and others is an expectation of their gender, and thus, competence in this "humor reading skill" would be more likely to increase someone's self-understanding. However, if this skill is considered not gender-appropriate, humor competence may not be related to a boy's sense of self-understanding.

The findings reviewed in this chapter suggest that complex connections across time (similarities and differences) exist among different dimensions of ToM, humor perceptions in self and other and self-perceptions. Such findings support previous research (Cutting & Dunn, 1999; Jenkins & Astington, 1996), and theorists' claims that self-perceptions and humor perception may play significant roles in children's ToM understanding (Bruner, 1996; Gergen, 2001; Harre, 1986; 1978).

Regarding individual differences in children's humor understanding and self-perception scores, perhaps girls are more likely to understand mental states in others were also more capable of perceiving humor in of others in middle childhood as Bosacki (2013) found. Regarding perceiving humor in oneself, perhaps girls scored higher than boys at 10 years of age because of societal messages that encourage females to remain positive and maintain a sense of humor to please others and may be more likely to engage in self-defeating humor (Hampes, 2004; Tannen, 1994; Layard & Dunn, 2009; Walker, 2005). As outlined in the next section, these findings support past research that suggests that children's higher ToM abilities may lead them to imagine both the positive and negative interior worlds of others (Hughes, 2011).

Regarding gender-related findings on ToM and humor perceptions, based on past research (Bosacki, 2013), compared to males, perhaps some females who are more likely to understand mental states in others are also more capable of perceiving humor in self and others in the middle childhood and early adolescent years. Given that gender may be considered as a culture (Maccoby, 1998), such gender-related differences may be in part due to societal cultural messages that encourage females to remain positive and maintain a sense of humor to please others (Tannen, 1994; Layard & Dunn, 2009; Walker, 2005). As outlined in the next section, these findings provide implications for future research that explores how adolescents' advanced ToM abilities may lead them to imagine both positive and negative interior worlds of others (Hughes, 2011).

5. APPLICATIONS

5.1. Practice

Regarding the practical applications of humor and ToM research, how do we develop educational programs that aim to connect our technological advancements with our moral and spiritual developments as humans such as our capacity for the radical acceptance of compassion and loving kindness (Brach, 2009; Keltner, 2009; Miller, 2010; Neff, 2011)? How well equipped are schools and educators to help adolescents learn how to negotiate the morally ambiguous global socio-cultural landscape, and how does this translate to developing inclusive programs that incorporate aspects of humor and ToM to help adolescents to negotiate the ambiguities both within the self, and relationships in the classroom, home, and larger community? For example, as recent research shows that resilient youth use humor to enhance socioemotional functioning during a day in the life of an adolescent (Cameron, Fox, Anderson & Cameron, 2010), researchers and educators need to explore how to incorporate aspect of humor into educational programs as this could have implications for emotional literacy and moral, inclusive education.

As I discussed earlier, we can build on such existing educational programs to help adolescents to develop a sense of awe and wonder in their everyday learning experiences.

For example, how we encourage youth to see the good in others, to focus on the positive events in their life by helping them to develop the necessary cognitive and emotional tools to frame their experiences as meaningful and exciting opportunities to grow and learn? Such possibilities are exciting in that educators and researchers can work together to create compassionate and caring classroom environments (Boorn, Hopkins- Dunn, & Page, 2010).

Such holistic educational programs need to draw on current research findings on the interpretation of ambiguity such as Yuill's (2009) research on jokes and riddles. More specifically, Yuill's (2009) findings suggested that supporting children to articulate multiple meanings was associated with improvements in comprehension. According to Yuill, joking riddles provide an excellent example of how different contexts support or cue different meanings, and this point was underlined by the association between comprehension improvement and utterances expressing both meanings of an ambiguity. The ways in which children expressed such utterances combining cued and uncued meanings suggest an impressive facility with language, and this was shown across a variety of different ambiguities.

Drawing on past research described earlier (McGhee, 1984), the strength or value of a joke could be dependent on the fact that it cues a particular context to give meaning to a phrase, but that the answer to the joke requires a different context to be understood. As Casteel (1997) suggests, it may not be enough just for children to know that words and multiple meanings, they need to understand how particular interpretations are required to fit different contexts. For example, graphic illustrations of jokes or ambigrams or puns could be used to encourage youth to 'play' with and to make meaning of ambiguous drawings and text (Bosacki, 2013). Such activities could be applied various academic disciplines such as math, science, and language arts to encourage adolescents to work on creating their own ambigrams. Complex cognitive skills such as divergent thinking and perspective taking are necessary to help adolescents to develop a sense of understanding the mental and emotional worlds of others and themselves. As many social cognitive researchers with youth attest (Bosacki, 2013; Masten, 1986), such cognitive competencies would hold potential value for adolescents living with our increasingly culturally diverse global context.

To start, educators and researchers can work together to co-create programs with the shared goals of aiming to help adolescents to develop a healthy sense of self, personal meaning, kindness and compassion toward others. For example, as I discussed above, to help adolescents navigate the ambiguous world of identity and relationships, educational programs need to incorporate psychoeducational models that promote well-being and mindful self-compassion including positive self-talk or caring private speech (Gibson, 2009; Neff, 2011).

As we develop and grow an inclusive and respectful classroom – one that integrates empirical evidence from studies on ToM and humor into the curriculum to promote well-being, we need to develop programs that help adolescents to learn to make sense of personal and social ambiguities in the classroom. Educators can serve as role models and help support the creation of creating a nurturing, psychological safe learning culture, one that cultivates a sense of meaning and purpose. That is, through the use of humor, adolescents may begin to feel psychologically safe enough to share and discuss personal and social stories of growth and resilience.

Such social cognitive approaches that focus on self-control and discipline as well as educational programs including Neff's (2011) work that fosters self-compassion supports similar educational programs that promote resilience and developing competencies to create healthy and effective coping strategies to make healthy life-style changes (Damon, 2008; McGrath & Nobel, 2009; Seligman, 2011). Educators suggest the need for further psychological and counseling support for youth in secondary school to help adolescents make healthy lifestyle choices, and for families to become active in learning processes among youth. Such programs promote the need for collaborative and team-based approaches to a youth's learning journey by encouraging partnerships among the student, parent, peer, and educator within the larger community. As I discussed at the beginning of this chapter, support from significant others as well as developing a youth's sense of agency and competency will help youth to learn effective and ambiguity with the goal of developing self, social, and cultural competence.

Humor as Content and Process within Secondary Schools. As already noted earlier in this chapter, past research has focused on humor in the classroom as either curriculum content, or within relationships and social interactions among teacher-student and peer-peer. Given recent research on geltophobia and self-perceptions, as Fuhr et al., (2015) suggest, future research should investigate the relation between gelotophobia and the use of humor for coping with adversity in adolescents. Educators may help youth to learn how to effectively deal with humor and laughter—and, especially, the usage of humor to cope with adversities such as social exclusion, bullying, among others.

As I have argued earlier, adolescence is a period of transition. These changes bring many opportunities for being laughed at and thus may place such targeted adolescents at higher risk of experiencing negative emotions such as humiliation, depression, and anxiety. Future research should study how adolescents can learn how to use humor to cope with life stressors, particularly school-related.

Given past research, adults and adolescents differ in the respect to the interplay between ToM, self-perceptions, and the use of humor to cope with adversities. It may be possible that adolescents who develop a humor coping style eventually become socially competent adults, and lose the fear of being laughed at, as they learn how to reinforce the benefits of humor-style coping over time. Unfortunately, to date, to the best of my knowledge, their remains a lack of longitudinal data on ToM, self-perceptions, humor perceptions, and gelotophobia, so developmental processes are at the level of speculation only. Such studies may provide a valuable starting point for the development of intervention programes for the promotion of humor as an emotional coping strategy to deal with negative emotions and challenging social situations.

Although the direction of causality between ToM, self-perceptions, and humor cannot be determined from existing data, as Fuhr et al., suggest (2015), perhaps young people with a higher self-acceptance may possess more confidence and courage to engage in meaningful social interaction (Ruch & Proyer, 2008a; Titze, 2009). Hence, as mentioned earlier, educational programs for youth that address emotion and humor understanding, self-acceptance, and compassion may be helpful. For example, educational programs could help youth to learn how to understand facial expressions and emotions experienced by others during social interactions within the classroom. In addition, educators could promote the use of fiction novels and comics within the classroom that integrate the use of humor into their text. Thus, such texts and comics may also help to provide youth with ideas to use humor as a way of coping with negative social situations or negative self-cognitions.

5.2. Future Research

Computer-Mediated Communication of CMC refers to the recent research area on digital discourse within the context of text-rich online environments. For example, discussion forums, blogs, and chats, humorous concepts need to be expressed without the aid of vocal tone, nonverbal gestures, facial expressions, or other visual and auditory cues of humor that are important performance variables in face-to-face communication (Garcia & Jacobs, 1999; Hancock 2004a). Overlapping messages or simultaneous feedback, typical of face-to-face interactions, are difficult to practice in real life situations (Fuchs, 2012).

Further, in several online environments, critical interactional variables such as gender, age, or social status remain unknown, due to the use of nicknames, avatars, or anonymous messages (Norrick & Chiaro, 2009).

Research shows that interactions in asynchronous computer-mediated environments, such as discussion online groups and forums, can provide an incentive for metalinguistic reflection and foster the formation and use of emergent instruments of expression (e.g., emoticons, abbreviations, graphics) that transform the online space into a dynamic stage for creative communication and language play (Thurlow et al., 2004; Herring, 2013). Such an interactive and dialogic context may encourage an extensive use of humor in online social spaces. Within this setting, Hancock (2004b) found that the participants in an experimental group, who interacted through CMC in a chat, were more likely to use more irony to accomplish specific conversational tasks than the participants in the control group, who communicated face-to-face. In general, research shows that the use of humor in CMC may help some individuals to overcome anonymity and reduce the sense of temporal and spatial separation (Baym, 1995).

The challenge for neuroscience researchers and educators for the next few decades will be to apply neuroscientific research findings to the digital classroom to show how modern technology may influence young people's developing minds. As Meece (2011) notes, we need to figure out how to cope and manage effectively with the current deluge of digital technology. We need to help adolescents to make healthy choices regarding their use of technological tools to promote their learning. As many researchers of adolescent's digital worlds discuss (Turkle, 2015), new technologies offer youth continuous stimuli that may pose new challenges for concentrated and focused learning.

A vast amount of research exists on the role of peer discussion in learning, as much of it based on Vygotskyan ideas. For instance, Vygotsky (1930/1978) argued that cognitive development occurs through social interaction, and that this development is mediated by language. Higher mental processes such as comprehension first appear through dialogue with others, and the language of these dialogues becomes internalized as private speech or self-talk. Several recent intervention programs in reading comprehension incorporate peer tutoring and the use of humor as a coping tool to manage anxiety-filled, stressful, and challenging personal and social experiences during adolescence (see Damon, 2008). Such programs may challenge young people to further their own understanding of humor within a social context, and to make elaborated explanations to their peers.

Regarding educational implications, although educators may find it a challenge to help any child or adolescent to develop humor-related skills, Markovits and Bowker's (2015) findings suggest that programs that help anxious-withdrawn young adolescents (especially boys) to develop humor-related coping styles could be critically important to develop supportive peer relationships. Fostering humor in anxious-withdrawn adolescents could also help them to cope more adaptively with stress and their fears and anxieties. Past research supports this claim, given findings that suggest humor is a common coping strategy during adolescence (Fuhr, 2002), as well as a highly effective coping strategy when dealing with stressful situations.

CONCLUSION

Although research on adolescents' humor and theory of mind has advanced, much remains to be done. In addition to measurement issues, the two fields are in need of cross-cultural and multidisciplinary longitudinal studies to elucidate the etiological pathways more effectively and to explore directly the implications for therapy and education. Finally, researchers are investigating humor and ToM within an increasingly expanding connected global social community. The meaning and implications of humor as content and process and how it connects to young people's ToM vary considerably across cultural contexts. Additionally, the continued emergence of digital technologies intended to connect us more easily and quickly to social and informational online networks raises questions about the very nature of humor and social communication.

Future research could continue to explore online humor as a means for adaptive coping strategies to deal with negative emotions such as depression and anxiety, or stressful interpersonal challenges. For example, a recent study explored the uses and functions of humor in an online community of video gamers and nonprofessional game designers (Marone, 2015). Marone found that online humor served as a community building 'cushioning glue' that fostered personal connections and social cohesion with peers. Marone's findings that participants used humor as a cohesive instrument to help build positive interpersonal relationships challenges the superiority theory of humor (Martineau, 1972). In contrast to Marone, Martineu would claim that the main role or function of humor within interpersonal relationships would include the use of power relations to apply criticism and create negative interpersonal relations. Given these contradictory findings, future studies need to continue to explore the role of online humor for adolescents and youth who experience shyness and social anxiety.

As noted earlier, research on adolescents' humor and theory of mind has advanced although much remains to be done. In addition to measurement issues, the two fields are in need of cross-cultural and multidisciplinary longitudinal studies to elucidate the etiological pathways more effectively and to explore directly the implications for therapy and education. Finally, the investigation of humor and ToM is increasingly expanding to the connected global social community.

The meaning and implications of humor as content and process, and how it connects to young people's ToM vary considerably across cultural contexts. Additionally, the continued emergence of digital technologies intended to connect us more easily and quickly to social and informational online networks raises questions about the very nature of humor and social communication. As research on humor and theory of mind continues, interdisciplinary, mixed-method, cross-cultural developmental studies need to elucidate the precise nature of cognitive and social influences on social cognition. Such studies will help to identify the mechanisms through which individual differences in theory of mind and humor production and reception affect adolescents' personal and social lives.

With research on children's ToM, self-concept, and humor perceptions still in its infancy, this chapter provides a starting point for future research on ToM understanding to include observational measures in naturalistic settings such as discourse analysis of peer conversations and playful talk on the playground, parent-child/ child-sibling conversations, among others. Moreover, given the complex process of emotion socialization, other factors not discussed in the present chapter may influence ToM understanding and perceptions of self and conversations (e.g., SES, gender of siblings, exposure to literature that focuses on mental states).

Research also shows that conversational and playful, possibly humorous experiences with friends and family, teachers and parents can help to promote ToM and humor perception as these are valuable social skills for the adolescent, regardless of one's gender or ethnicity. Thus, future research needs to investigate additional socialization agents who may influence the development and self-presentation of humor and humor perceptions, and emotional competence, including peers, teachers, family members, as well as the influence of media experiences with text (paper, electronic), social media, television, film, (Bosacki, 2013).

In sum, this chapter suggests that future research needs to explore older children's and adolescents' ToM, their perceived selves, and how they think and feel about humor as content. Studies also need to investigate perceptions of owning a 'sense of humor,' or being labelled by others as a 'funny person.' The ideas presented within this chapter may further the discourse on ToM development by highlighting the complexity of young people's socioemotional and sociolinguistic experiences during the transition from late childhood to adolescence, particularly regarding humor perception and styles, and gendered perceptions of cultural-identity. Overall, in support of recent claims from other developmental psychoeducators and sociolinguists (Davies, 2015; Dunn, 2008; Hughes, 2011), this chapter suggests the need for further investigation of the links between ToM understanding and the understanding of, and creation of humor.

REFERENCES

Amsterlaw, J., Lagatutta, K., & Meltzoff, A. (2009). Young children's reasoning about the effects of emotional and physiological states on academic performance. *Child Development, 80,* 15- 133.

Artar, M. (2007). Adolescent egocentrism and theory of mind in the context of family relations. *Social Behavior and Personality, 35,* 1211-1220.

Astington, J., & Pelletier, J. (1997, April). *Young children's theory of mind and its relation to their success in school.* Paper presented at the Biennial Meeting of the Society for Research in Child Development, Washington, DC.

Banerjee, M., & Yuill, N. (1999). Children's understanding of self-presentational display rules: Associations with mental-state understanding. *British Journal of Developmental Psychology, 17,* 111-124.

Banerjee, R., Watling, D., & Caputi, M. (2011). Peer relations and understanding of faux pas: Longitudinal evidence for bidirectional associations. *Child Development, 82,* 1887–1905.

Baron-Cohen, S. (2011). *The science of evil: On empathy and the origins of cruelty.* New York: Basic Books.

Baym, N. K. (1995). 'The performance of humour in computer-mediated communication.' *Journal of Computer-Mediated Communication* 1 (2), p. 0.

Berger, A. (2013)/ 'Forty five ways to make 'em laugh. *Israeli Journal of Humor Research, 1,* 45-57.

Bosacki, S. (2015). Children's theory of mind, self-perceptions, and peer relations: A longitudinal study. *Infant and Child Development, 24,* 175-188. DOI: 10.1002/icd.1878.

Bosacki, S. (2013). A longitudinal study of children's Theory of Mind, self-concept, and perceptions of humor in self and other. *Social Behavior and Personality, 41,* 663-674.

Bosacki, S. (2008). *Children's emotional lives: Sensitive shadows in the classroom.* New York: Peter Lang.

Bosacki, S. (2003). Psychological pragmatics in preadolescents: Sociomoral understanding, self-worth, and school behavior. *Journal of Youth and Adolescence, 32,* 141-155.

Bosacki, S. (2000). Theory of mind and self-concept in preadolescents: Links with gender and language. *Journal of Educational Psychology, 92,* 709-717.

Bosacki, S., & Astington, J. (1999). Theory of mind in preadolescence: Relations between social understanding and social competence. *Social Development, 8, 237-255.*

Bronfenbrenner, U. (1977). Toward an experimental ecology of human development. *American Psychologist, 32,* 513-531.

Bruner, J. (1996). *The culture of education.* Cambridge, MA: Harvard University Press.

Bussey, K., & Bandura, A. (1999). Social cognitive theory of gender development and differentiation. *Psychological Review, 106,* 676-713.

Caravita, S., Di Biasio, P., & Salmivalli, C. (2010). Early adolescents' participation in bullying: Is ToM involved? *The Journal of Early Adolescence, 30,* 138-170.

Carpendale, J., & Chandler, M. J. (1996). On the distinction between false belief understanding and subscribing to an interpretive theory of mind. *Child Development, 67,* 1686-1706.

Carpendale, J., & Lewis, C. (2004). Constructing an understanding of mind: The development of children's social interaction within social interaction. *Behavioral and Brain Sciences, 27,* 79–151.

Cassidy, J., Ross, D., Butkovsky, L., & Braungart, J. (1992). Family-peer connections: The roles of emotional expressiveness within the family and children's understanding of emotions. *Child Development, 63,* 603-618.

Creswell, J. W. (2011). *Educational research: Planning, conducting, and evaluating quantitative and qualitative research.* (4th Ed.). Upper Saddle River, NJ: Merrill Prentice Hall.

Cushman F. (2008). Crime and punishment: Distinguishing the roles of causal and intentional analyses in moral judgment. *Cognition, 108*(2), 353-380.

Cutting, A., & Dunn, J. (2002). The costs of understanding other people: social cognition predicts young children's sensitivity to criticism. *Journal of Child Psychology and Psychiatry, 43,* 849-860.

Damon, W., & Hart, D. (1988*). Self-understanding in childhood and adolescence.* New York: Cambridge University Press.

de Rosnay, M., & Hughes, C. (2006). Conversation and theory of mind: Do children talk their way to socio-cognitive understanding? *British Journal of Developmental Psychology, 24*, 7-37.

Davies, C. (2015). Humor in intercultural interaction as both content and process in the classroom. *Humor, 28*, 375-395.

Devine, R. T., & Hughes, C. (2013). Silent films and strange stories: Theory of mind, gender, and social experiences in middle childhood. *Child Development, 84*, 989–1003.

Dunn, J. (1995). Children as psychologists: The later correlates of individual differences in understanding of emotions and other minds. *Emotion and Cognition, 9*, 187-201.

Dunn, J. (2008). Relationships and children's discovery of the mind. In U. Muller, N. Budwig, & B. Sokol., (Eds.), *Social life and social knowledge: Toward a process account of development* (pp. 171-182). New York: Lawrence Erlbaum Associates.

Dunn, J., Brown, J., Slomkowski, C., Tesla, C., & Youngblade, L. (1991). Young children's understanding of other people's feelings and beliefs: Individual differences and their antecedents. *Child Development, 62*, 1352–1366.

Dunn, L., & Dunn, L. (1997). *Peabody Picture Vocabulary Test* (Third Edition). Circle Pines, MN: American Guidance Service.

Fiasee, C. & Nader-Grosbois, N. (2012). Perceived social acceptance, theory of mind, and children with intellectual disabilities. *Research in Developmental Disabilities, 33*, 1871-1880.

Filoppova, E., & Astington, J. (2008). Further developments in social reasoning revealed in discourse irony understanding. *Child Development, 79*, 126-138.

Filoppova, E., & Astington, J. (2010). Children's understanding of social-cognitive and social-communicative aspects of discourse irony. *Child Development, 81*, 913-928.

Führ, M. (2002). 'Coping humour in early adolescence.' *Humour: International Journal of Humour Research* 15, 283-304.

Fuhr, M., Platt, & Proyer, R. (2015). Testing the relations of gelotopia with humour as a coping strategy, self-ascribed loneliness, reflectivity, attractiveness, self-acceptance, and life expectations. *European Journal of Humour Research, 3*, 84-97.

Gergen, M. (2001). *Feminist reconstructions in psychology*. Sage, Thousand Oaks, CA.

Hampes, W. (2006). Humor and shyness: The relation between humor styles and shyness. *Humor The International Journal of Humor Research*, 19(2), 179–187. doi:10.1515/HUMOR.2006.009.

Hancock, J. T. (2004a). 'LOL: Humour online.' *ACM Interactions*, 11, 57-58.

Hancock, J. T. (2004b). 'Verbal irony use in face-to-face and computer-mediated conversations.' *Journal of Language and Social Psychology*, 23, 447-463.

Harter, S. (1985). *Manual for the self-perception profile for children (SPPC)*. University of Denver.

Harter, S. (1999). *The construction of the self: A developmental perspective*. New York: Guilford Press.

Hughes, C. (2011). *Social understanding and social lives: From toddlerhood through to the transition to school*. New York: Psychology Press.

Hughes, C., & Devine, R. T. (2015). A social perspective on theory of mind. In M. Lamb & C. Garcia-Coll (Eds.), *Handbook of child psychology and developmental science* (Vol. 3, 7th ed., pp. 564–609). Hoboken, NJ: Wiley.

Hughes, C., & Dunn, J. (1998). Theory of mind and emotion understanding: Longitudinal associations with mental-state talk between young friends. *Developmental Psychology, 34*, 1026-1037.

Hughes, C., Jaffee, S. R., Taylor, A., Caspi, A., & Moffitt, T. E. (2005). Origins of individual differences in theory of mind: From nature to nurture? *Child Development, 76*, 356–370.

Jasper, J. (2011). Talking like a 'zerolingual': Ambiguous linguistic caricatures at an urban secondary school. *Journal of Pragmatics, 43*(5), 1264-1278.

Kielar-Turska, M., & Bialecka-Pikul, M. (2009). Generating and understanding jokes by five-and nine-year old as an expression of Theory of Mind. *Polish Psychological Bulletin, 40*, 163-169.

Kim, J. (2014). How Korean EFL learners understand sarcasm in L2 English. *Journal of Pragmatics, 60*, 193-206.

Klein, D. N., & Kupier, N. A. (2006). Humor styles, peer relationships, and bullying in middle childhood. *Humor The International Journal of Humor Research, 19*(4), 383–404. doi:10.1515/ HUMOR.2006.019.

Knack, J. M., Tsar, V., Vaillancourt, T., Hymel, S., & McDougal, P. (2012). What protects rejected adolescents from also being bullied by their peers? The moderating role of peer-valued characteristics. *Journal of Research on Adolescence, 22*(3), 467–479. doi:10.1111/j.1532-7795.2012.00792.x.

Lagattuta, K. H., Sayfan, L., & Harvey, C. (2014). Beliefs about thought probability: Evidence for persistent errors in mindreading and links to executive control. *Child Development, 85*, 659–674.

Layard, R., & Dunn, J. (2009). *A good childhood: Searching for values in a competitive age.* London, UK: Penguin.

Lecce, S., & Hughes, C. (2010). "The Italian job?" Comparing theory of mind performance in British and Italian children. *British Journal of Developmental Psychology, 28*, 747-766.

Lecce, S., Caputi, M., & Hughes, C. (2011). Does sensitivity to criticism mediate the relationship between theory of mind and academic competence? *Journal of Experimental Child Psychology, 110*, 313-331.

Lecce, S., Bianco, F., Devine, R. T., Hughes, C., & Banerjee, R. (2014). Promoting theory of mind during middle childhood: A training program. *Journal of Experimental Child Psychology, 126*, 52–67.

Leekam, S. (1993). Children's understanding of mind. In M. Bennett (Ed.), *The child as psychologist: An introduction to the development of social cognition* (pp. 191-198). New York: Harvester Wheatsheaf.

Lewis, C., Freeman, N. H., Kyriakidou, C., Maridaki-Kassotaki, K., & Berridge, D. M. (1996).

Social influences on false belief access: Specific sibling influences or general apprenticeship? *Child Development, 67*, 2930–2947. doi:10.2307/1131760.

Lundgen, K., & Brownell, H. (2015). Selective training of Theory of Mind in Traumatic Brain Injury: A series of single subject training studies. *The Open Behavioral Science Journal, 9*, 1-11.

Markovic, A., & Bowker, J. (2015). Shy, but Funny? Examining peer-valued characteristics as moderators of the associations between anxious-withdrawal and peer outcomes during early adolescence. *Journal of Youth and Adolescence, 44*, 833-846.

Marone, V. (2015). Online humour as a community-building glue. *European Journal of Humour Research, 3*, 61-83.

Martineau, W. H. (1972). 'A model of the social functions of humour,' in Goldstein, J.H., & McGhee, P.E. (eds.), *The Psychology of Humour: Theoretical Perspectives and Empirical Issues,* New York: Academic Press, pp. 101-125.

McAlister, A., & Peterson, C. (2007). A longitudinal study of child siblings and theory of mind development. *Cognitive Development, 22*, 258–270. doi:10.1016/j.cogdev.2006.10.009.

Meins, E., Fernyhough, C., Johnson, F., & Lidstone, J. (2006). Mind-mindedness in children: Individual differences in internal-state talk in middle childhood. *British Journal of Developmental Psychology, 24,* 181–196. doi:10.1348/026151005X80174.

Maccoby, E. (1998). *The two sexes: Growing up apart, coming together.* Cambridge, MA: Harvard University Press.

Martin, R. A. (2007). *The psychology of humor: An integrative approach.* London: Academic Press.

Marone, V. (2015). *Online humour as a community-building cushioning glue.* European Journal of Humour Research, 3, 61-83.

Martin, R. A., Puhlik-Doris, P., Larsen, G., Gray, J., & Weir, K. (2003). Individual differences in uses of humor and their relation to psychological well-being: development of the humor styles questionnaire. *Journal of Research in Personality, 37,* 48e75, doi:10.1016/S0092-6566(02)00534-2.

Nucci, L. (2009). *Nice is not enough: Facilitating moral development.* Upper Saddle River, NJ: Pearson.

Oberle, E., Schonert-Reichl, K., Stewart Lawlor, M., & Thomson, K. (2011). Mindfulness and inhibitory control in early adolescence, *The Journal of Early Adolescence, 30,* 125-136. doi:10.1177/0272431611403741.

Lagatutta, K., & Wellman, H. M. (2002). Differences in early parent-child conversations about negative versus positive emotions. *Developmental Psychology, 38,* 564–580.

Pons, F., Lawson, J., Harris, Pl., & de Rosnay, M. (2003). Individual differences in children's emotion understanding: Effects of age and language. *Scandinavian Journal of Psychology, 44,* 347-411.

Pons, F., Harris, P. L., & de Rosnay, M. (2004). Emotion comprehension between 3 and 11 years: Developmental periods and hierarchical organization. *European Journal of Developmental Psychology, 2(1),* 127–152.

Proyer, R. Meier, I., Platt, T., & Ruch, W. (2013). Dealing with laughter and ridicule in adolescence: Relations with bullying and emotional responses. *Social Psychology of Education: An International Journal, 16,* 399-420.

Salovey, P., & Sluyter, D. (1997). *Emotional development and emotional intelligence: Educational implications.* New York: Basic Books.

Samson, A. C. The influence of empathizing and systemizing on humor processing: theory of mind and humor. *Humor: International Journal of Humor Research,* in press.

Samson, A. C., & Hegenloh, M. (2010). Structural stimulus properties affect humor processing in individuals with Asperger syndrome. *Journal of*

Autism and Developmental Disorders, 40, 438e447, doi:10.1007/s10803-009-0885-2.

Samsona, S., Lacknerb,H, Weissd, E., & Papousekd, I. (2012). Perception of other people's mental states affects humor in social anxiety. *Journal of Behavior Therapy and Experimental Psychology, 43,* 625-631.

Seligman, M. (2011). *Flourish.* New York: Free Press.

Siegel, D. (2013). *Brainstorm: The power and purpose of the teenage brain.* New York: Jeremy Tarcher/Penguin.

Sutton, J., Smith, P., & Swettenham, J. (1999). Bullying and 'theory of mind'; a critique of the 'social skills deficit' view of anti-social behaviour. *Social Development, 8,* 117-127.

Tannen, D. (1994). *Gender and discourse.* New York: Oxford University Press.

Turkle, S. (2015). *Reclaiming conversation: The power of talk in a digital age.* Penguin Press: New York.

Walker, S. (2005). Gender differences in the relationship between young children's peer-related social competence and individual differences in theory of mind. *Journal of Genetic Psychology, 166,* 297-312.

Watson, A., Nixon, C., Wilson, A., & Capage, L. (1999). Social interaction skills and theory of mind in young children. *Developmental Psychology, 35,* 386-391.

Yuill, N., & Coultas, J. (2007, June). *The relation between emotion recognition and social experience in early adolescence.* Poster presented at the annual meeting of the Jean Piaget Society, Amsterdam, ND.

In: Humor   ISBN: 978-1-63484-787-2
Editor: Holly Phillips   © 2016 Nova Science Publishers, Inc.

Chapter 5

COMPLEXITY AND CHAOS: ORGANIZATIONAL HUMOR AND EMOTIONS

Barbara Plester·
University of Auckland, Business School,
Auckland, New Zealand

ABSTRACT

Humor is pervasive, has been described as ubiquitous, and plays an important role in many social interactions. A seminal social context for many people is that of their workplace or perhaps key organizations in which they associate, volunteer or belong. Organizational contexts can be fraught with tension, stress and difficulties and humor can help mitigate some of these aspects.

Drawing upon several years of empirical, ethnographic research, this chapter examines the role of humor in easing organizational relationships that are influenced by issues such as hierarchy, power, control, and diversity. Team and group configurations are prominent and widespread in organizations and humor can ease group interactions, foster collegiality and goodwill and create positive emotions at work (see Cooper, 2005, 2008). Contrastingly, humor is also used in less salubrious ways and it can create dissension, disharmony and foster negative emotions. Although not readily acknowledged, humor does have a dark side and this

---

· b.plester@auckland.ac.nz.

less-popular aspect of the humor construct is not well-researched and examined (see Billig, 2005).

Physiological research suggests that humor can have beneficial effects upon health and the most consistent findings suggest that humor can help to reduce pain and boost immunity systems (Martin, 2007). What is more commonly agreed is that humor plays a key role in promoting mental health and well-being through acting as a coping technique for stress and tension and this specific attribute is particularly useful in high-stress work contexts. Therefore this chapter will explore some of the ways that humor may influence workplace health and well-being, while also addressing some of the problematic aspects of humor use.

Using empirical examples, this chapter will emphasize that humor is complex, ambiguous and can cause both happy, positive emotions as well as negative, destructive feelings in organizational life. Humor can even elicit happy, cheerful, merriment and problematic discord - simultaneously - which can create confusion, ambivalence and even chaos in extreme cases. Therefore simply attempting to co-opt humor as an organizational tool or device is not a simple strategy that is easily implemented and enacted. Understanding the multiplicity of functions, uses and forms of humor is a more realistic starting point for recognizing the emotive social power of humor.

INTRODUCTION

Although the positive psychology movement frequently includes studies that highlight the positive aspects and functions of humor use, they tend to neglect the negative aspects of humor and these are under-investigated and somewhat neglected in humor literature. This chapter attempts to offer a broader perspective of the role of humor in emotion, health and social interactions and investigates both positive and negative dimensions of humor and its effects.

A sense of humor involves several aspects and scholars have struggled to create a universal definition for the concept. Humor is complex, nuanced ambiguous and paradoxical and can be viewed in a variety of ways. It can be interpreted as a stimulus to create amusement and/or laughter; a reaction to something funny; or as a disposition -as in 'being of good humor' (Chapman & Foot, 1976). A definition from psychological humor research claims that humor is a *process* initiated by a *stimulus* (such as a joke) resulting in a *response* (such as laughter) indicating pleasure (Godkewitsch, 1976). This definition does however, ignore the dark side of humor and it is possible for a situation, quip or event to be funny while also being offensive and upsetting and creating negative emotions. This chapter will examine both positive and negative emotions linked to humor as both are significant in humor analyses - although the extant research tends to overemphasize benefits and positive emotions such as happiness, enthusiasm and joy. Emotions such as anger and disgust are highly relevant in humor events and the chapter will offer a variety of examples to illustrate the wide range of emotions found in humor enactments.

The study of emotion is a relatively new field (Lively, 2006), there are as many theories of emotion as there are theorists, and a universal theory of emotion may not be achievable (Ashkanasy, Härtel & Zerbe, 2000). The only general consensus appears to support the notion that 'emotion is a syndrome- a pattern of co-occurring responses' (Ashkanasy et al., 2000: 11). Processes that must be considered in relation to emotion are those of cognition, physiological changes, emotional displays and feeling states or moods (Ashkanasy et al., 2000). Although there are differences between scholars as to the range and number of basic emotions it is commonly agreed that there are six basic emotions which include: happiness, sadness, fear, surprise, anger and disgust (Ekman, 1992). Ekman. (1992) also lists a comprehensive range of emotions that include (in alphabetical order): 'anger, awe, contempt, disgust, embarrassment, excitement, fear, guilt, interest, sadness, shame, and surprise' He also discusses enjoyment which he asserts is 'comprised of at least amusement, contentment, relief, enjoyment from sensory sources, and enjoyment based on accomplishment' (Ekman, 1992: 193). Ekman goes on to suggest that the emotions of contempt, shame, guilt, embarrassment and awe share the same characteristics as the aforementioned six basic emotions. Furthermore, Ekman asserts that the primary purpose of emotions is to mobilise humans to deal with 'interpersonal encounters' (p. 171) and thus this chapter examines the role of humor in relational interactions.

HUMOR IS USED TO MANAGE EMOTIONS

It is broadly believed that humor can positively affect physical health, well-being and people's mental condition (Astedt-Kurki, Isola, Tammentie & Kervinen, 2001) and that humor is a 'powerful antidote to negative emotions' (Samson & Gross, 2012: 375). Humor is mostly experienced as enjoyable and pleasurable as it allows people to 'express strong emotions' (Martin, 2007: 57). The useful physiological and psychological effects are generated through laughter which can reflect emotions such as mirth, embarrassment or joy. Conversely humor can also be used to express negative emotions and can contain destructive elements such as mocking, disdain and aimed barbs (Billig, 2005).

Adopting a Freudian perspective, humor may be experienced as a relief or release, and thus humor can offer an outlet for emotions that may be difficult to express in other ways. In his book: *Jokes and the Unconscious* (1905), Sigmund Freud argues that humor allows people to express ideas or feelings that are not always socially expressed, particularly sentiments related to sex or aggression. Thus humor is a permitted device or a socially acceptable way to express socially taboo impulses and the release of these types of ideas through humor is cathartic and a useful way to blow off steam (Martin, 2007). It has even been suggested that when people use humor to release strong emotions this is a socially useful role as it creates social harmony and avoids the expression of real emotions that may cause problems (Douglas, 1999).

Nursing studies show that humor can be used to reframe situations and relieve tension. An originally distressing or frustrating situation can be reframed using humor which offers a coping strategy for those involved (Dean & Major, 2008). Samson and Gross suggest that positive humor, which they define as humor that is good-natured, kind and lacks hostility, can enable people to reframe a negative event and distract people from the negative impacts of some events. Positive humor offers a 'reappraisal of the situation' (2012: 381) whereas although negative humor can help to create emotional distance from an upsetting event, it does not offer the ability to reframe it and see the 'bright side.' However these researchers concede that in truly awful, difficult, and life-threatening circumstances, negative forms of humor may be more helpful to cope with hardships and threats and reduce the tense and stressful emotions such situations invoke, therefore there is a contextual element to using humor to manage emotions. Humor has a unique capacity to help people express and transmit difficult, threatening or volatile messages which helps to reframe negative emotions as more acceptable (Carbelo & Jáuregui, 2006).

In a study of female sex workers, Sanders, (2004) found that these women use humor as 'emotion work' (p. 274) to help them cope with selling their bodies and the dangers of their working environment. Similarly, emergency workers and people who face danger or unpleasant, difficult work conditions use humor as a positive strategy to help them deal with tensions, stress, anxiety, trauma and fear (Alexander & Wells, 1991; Moran & Massam, 1997; Sanders, 2004;). Humor is a resistance strategy that offers people a way of coping with pain and humiliation because events can be reframed from painful episodes into funny stories that create an emotional distance for the participants or observers of the traumatic, difficult experience (Downe, 1999) and thus humor offers a psychological escape (Obrdlik, 1942). Humor that is expressed in the most trying of circumstances has come to be known as *gallows* humor (see Freud, 1927; Obdrlik, 1942). Gallows humor can help prevent despair and fend off suffering and trauma, offering a sort of liberation of the spirit in defiance of suffering and peril (Freud, 1927).

Although gallows humor refers to the most extreme forms of humor usually found in dire conditions, Freud also highlighted the power of humor to relieve everyday tensions and anti-social urges because it can allow unconscious urges to surface, creating a momentary feeling of freedom from societal restrictions and control (Bowers & Smith, 2004; Douglas, 1999). In general, people do control their sexual and aggressive impulses in society, but according to Freud, laughter can free people from their inhibitions and humor can assume a 'safety valve' function as it offers an overflow function for the 'disposal of redundant emotions' (Koestler, 1964: 62). Psychological humor researchers assert that using humor to let off steam in a safe way promotes collective accord and prevents anti-social behaviour that can cause outrage and offence. (Douglas, 1999; Freud, 1905; Gruner, 1997; Morreal, 1983; Weick & Westley, 1996; Wilson, 1979.) Furthermore, as argued by Freud (1905), the risqué and taboo aspects of sexual and/or aggressive humor creates even greater amusement and pleasure, is more memorable and enjoyable, and therefore offers a greater feeling of release for constrained emotions.

The following example demonstrates the release function of humor in a workplace setting. In this observed workplace interaction, a salesman (Alf) walks up to a group of colleagues and pointedly and loudly remarks to his co-worker Kara: *'you're a bitch!'* The assembled group all laugh heartily at the profane and aggressive insult, showing that they consider it a joke- which nominally it is. The background to the remark is that Alf had not been given tickets to a company movie night that Kara had organized and he was upset. Rather than making a formal complaint he framed his annoyance in a provocative and aggressive 'joke,' and thus Kara and the group all laugh at his pointed barb. By framing this as a joke, Alf is able to express his displeasure in a socially acceptable way while still making the firm point that Kara neglected him.

As he departs from the group Alf makes another pointed, joking remark declaring: *'Pete came through with tickets for me, but you're still a bitch!'* (In Plester, 2015a; Schnurr & Plester, 2016). This causes more laughter from everyone including Kara. Kara may not have liked being blatantly called a '*bitch*' but in using a wry tone and a large mocking grin, Alf makes it clear that this is a joke, albeit an aimed joke. In reframing his anger as a profane joke Alf releases his frustration, makes a fairly strong point and can openly express this under the protection of humor-it is 'just a joke.' Thus, as posited by Freud, the aimed or tendentious joke serves a useful purpose, allows the expression of strong emotion but at the same time avoids offence and disapproval through using 'joke work' (Freud, 1905: 61). Alf has the defence of 'just joking' which leaves Kara somewhat powerless to complain without looking like a poor sport who can't take a joke. Thus social harmony is maintained whilst Alf is able to express his feelings forcibly and lightly at the same time. In this instance the humor worked and Alf got the upper hand but humor such as this can be risky and cause offence and distress. When humor is perceived to have transgressed or 'gone too far' it can cause hostile reactions such as misery and outrage. For this humor to have been successfully enacted, Alf also had to be fairly sure of Kara's likely response and he ensured that the insult would be accepted as a joke by making his remark loudly, openly, in front of a group of people and with a beaming grin on his face and a jocular tone of voice. All of these contextual elements are important to the creation of the joke frame so that Alf's remarks are perceived as funny rather than blatantly hostile. Alf has successfully reframed his emotions of disappointment and annoyance (or anger) into an amusing jocular insult seemingly enjoyed by his co-workers.

HUMOR CREATES EMOTIONS

Although the previous section has focused upon how humor can allow people to manage and deal with emotions, it is significant that humor itself may be a catalyst for multiple different emotions - both positive and negative. On a global scale we have recently seen political humor cause such outrage and anger that it has resulted in extreme violence against the perceived protagonists in the Charlie Hedbo tragedy. A little less recently, a prank instigated by two Australian radio hosts backfired horrifically when British nurse Jacintha Saldhanha, took her own life in the aftermath of being publically humiliated by a prank created by the radio employees. The radio hosts tricked Ms Saldhanha into believing that they were members of the British Royal family checking on the welfare of Kate Middleton (Duchess of Cambridge) - who had been hospitalised with hyperemesis gravidarum. The radio hosts had assumed false British accents and laughingly broadcast their successful prank in Australia which subsequently received worldwide attention. After Ms. Saldhana's unexpected and horrifying death, the radio hosts were globally criticized (BBC News, 2012, 2014) and have since expressed their deep regret, guilt and remorse at creating such overwhelming emotions for their hapless victim.

Of course, humor does not always cause such humiliation and unhappiness. One of the things that is most enjoyable about humor is the range of pleasurable and positive emotions that can be engendered by the shared appreciation of a joke or funny experience. The majority of the extant humor research does focus on the positive aspects of humor and much research highlights the camaraderie, connection and warmth created between people who share humor. Research such as Cooper's relational process model (2008) and Fine and De Soucey's (2005) work on social integration shows that humor in groups can create positive feelings of inclusion, camaraderie and pleasure. The following workplace example shows how a work team uses humor to congratulate their boss and make him feel warmly appreciated and happy.

This financial organization held their annual 'Employee of the Year' awards and the recipient had previously been one of the 12 'Employee of the Month' winners during the year. The winner was a team manager called Brad* who was awarded travel vouchers and a trophy. The award was conveyed during a luxurious celebration including champagne and catered food. As the celebration was held at the end of the working day Brad and his team left for home after the festivities and everyone appeared happy about the celebration and Brad's well-deserved recognition. Early the next morning, the team that Brad managed arrived early at the office and using a vast quantity of toilet paper, proceeded to wrap up absolutely everything in Brad's work cubicle. Even the large items such as his chair, computer and desk were fully swathed. With much happy chuckling the team then resumed their usual work positions and with cameras at the ready, they waited for Brad to arrive. Unsuspecting, Brad walked into his workspace and stopped still in amazement at the sight of a fully wrapped cubicle. He laughed and laughed and was soon joined by his happy team who surrounded him, clapped him fondly on the back and seemed to thoroughly enjoy his amazed reaction. Surrounded by his team and their good wishes Brad shook his head and repeated in amazement: *'you guys... I can't believe you did this...you guys...'* (In Plester, 2015a).

A physical prank is always risky especially in a work context as it causes disruption to work activities and can upset and annoy some people. Although it took quite some time for Brad to unwrap all of his work tools and resume his tasks, he seemed delighted by the joke and interpreted it as his team's fondness and respect for him. The team members and this popular manager all emphasized that this joke had created warmth, inclusion and camaraderie for them as a team. Key to the success of this prank was the subordinates' knowledge of their manager, Brad, and their belief that he enjoyed humor and fun and would take the prank in good spirit. The loud and happy laughter attracted people from other areas of the workplace who walked over to see the spectacle and joined the laughter and bonhomie.

Although there are many similar examples of pranks such as this on the internet, the surprise and unexpectedness of the wrapped cubicle created humor and enjoyment for those involved as well as those viewing the result. *Incongruity* is considered to be a key element in most, if not all, humor and incongruity humor theories highlight cognitive elements of humor more than the social and emotional aspects (Martin, 2007). Humor can be created through the juxtaposition of competing ideas or through absurdity, unpredictability and irregularity in humorous enactments (Attardo, 1997; Duncan, Smeltzer & Leap, 1990; Fry & Allen, 1976; Wilson, 1979). The emotional elements are also significant and in a follow-up discussion Brad admitted that the prank had made him feel happy and valued by his team and it had reinforced their support of his award and created stronger team inclusiveness and cohesion. This team was proud of their ability to enjoy fun at work (a core value within the company) and the prank allowed the team members to show their respect for Brad's achievement without being overly sycophantic. Although Brad had been revered and elevated in his company by receiving a major award, this prank by his team reminded him that he could still be teased and restored the balance in the team social dynamics (see Smith, 2009). Although this prank worked out well, pranks can and sometimes do, go horribly wrong and create the opposite effect as to what may have been intended. The aforementioned radio host (Royal family) hoax exemplifies a case of a prank causing terrible humiliation with a tragic result. The next example is an ambivalent one as the prank did not specifically go wrong but it definitely had the potential for terrible repercussions and the extremity of this prank causes some different emotions in the participants.

In this workplace example (see Plester, 2015a) Kasey narrated a situation where she had been joking and teasing with her male colleagues inside the company warehouse where they all worked and packed products for customers. Kasey, a physically diminutive young woman in her twenties had been getting the better of the men she worked with by using her clever wit to tease and jokingly mock them. She was a reasonably recent addition to this work team. During the verbal repartee, quite suddenly, amid laughter and shouting, two of the men physically restrained Kasey and proceeded to tie her by her limbs and torso to the struts of a forklift. Once she was immobilized they then hoisted Kasey high into the air and teased that they would leave her there indefinitely and then they walked away. Eventually they returned, lowered the forklift and the abusive (but jocular) banter continued as they released Kasey amid much high-spirited laughter from the entire group-including Kasey. As she narrated the story, Kasey revealed that she was very afraid of heights and so the physical prank had scared her but at no point did she communicate this to her male co-workers and she did not reveal this to them afterwards. She 'took' the prank and laughed heartily as she recounted both the story and her genuine fear. Kasey admitted that she also felt pride that she had managed to conceal her strong emotions behind the joking banter and that in being singled out for this prank, she felt included and respected by her male colleagues. Kasey enjoyed telling her tale and her stoic endurance of the prank had given her the reputation of being 'tough' and 'one of the boys' (see Fine & De Soucey, 2005). Obviously there was great potential for injury, there were safety violations and the possibility that Kasey could become highly upset at being restrained, frightened and physically powerless. These emotions were all present for Kasey but interestingly the emotions of pride, inclusion, collegiality and acceptance were more important to her and she focused on these aspects of the incident rather than the potentially negative outcomes-which were significant. Because the incident was framed as humor and a 'joke' it may be that Kasey was compelled to laugh and treat this as funny otherwise she risked being seen as 'weak' 'female' and 'different' to her male co-workers. Gendered features of humor are another area of research and inquiry and in the workplace include aspects of power, control and domination that can create a whole raft of conflicting, ambiguous and complex emotions and this is an area that requires further in-depth research (see Plester, 2015 b).

This physical prank could be viewed as a type of 'hazing' similar to that experienced in environments such as the military or college fraternities. Although hazing is not fully understood, psychologists emphasize the creation of affiliation, solidarity and group identity engendered by such activities (Josefowitz & Gadon, 1989). Kasey's seemingly calm acceptance of the prank firmly embedded her as a team member and the framing of the incident as a 'joke' manipulates the target (Kasey) into interpreting it as fun and goodwill rather than dangerous and threatening. Furthermore, the joke frame protects (to some extent) the protagonists from reproaches but this is risky humor because had this gone wrong and had Kasey got hurt, organizational discipline and recriminations would have been swift and significant.

Although this was a risky humor incident, with gender issues, control, domination and safety violations, Kasey adamantly asserted that this was 'good fun' showing that she had framed this as a positive emotional experience. It seems as if the risky elements that she endured added to her emotional engagement and thus the joke has attained legendary status in Kasey's cognitive ascription as well as that of her workplace colleagues. This supports the Freudian premise (1905) that the riskier the humor the more funny and memorable the incident. This again illustrates the edgy nature of humor which poises on a knife-edge at times. The forbidden and dangerous aspects of this prank enhances the humor and increases the pleasure in re-telling the story. In this specific case, Kasey released her fear and anxiety through uninhibited laughter throughout the incident and also after it was over and in all of her subsequent narrations of her story.

Although it seems logical to separate humor experiences into positive and negative humor interactions, such a dichotomy is somewhat oversimplified and what is more usual is that humor creates a mixture of emotions simultaneously. Emotions may vary depending on the context, the people involved, and the different beliefs, customs and sensibilities of those either involved in, or witnessing the humor. It is even possible to involve all six of the basic emotions within the same instance or sequence of humor. Kasey's example illustrates feelings of fear and anxiety simultaneously occurring with surprise, happiness, and the pleasure she felt from inclusion and group bonding. The Australian radio prank firstly created amusement and pleasure at the trickery which quickly turned to disgust, horror and deep sadness at the resulting tragedy. Humor is complicated to understand and analyze (see Plester, 2015 a) and additionally creates a cornucopia of complex emotions, often concurrently. Therefore it is really difficult to point to specific health benefits arising from humor and although the positive psychology movement certainly aspires to establish a firm link between humor and good health- this is not easily accomplished. In fact, there is an equal and opposing argument that humor can also be bad for one's heath and cause misery, embarrassment and unhappiness (Billig, 2005). Billig asserts that the negative aspects of humor are under-researched and often overlooked because investigating humor that contains mockery and derision as well as associating humor with negative emotions and moods, is unpopular and results in accusations that one is a misogelast (laughter-hater) and a curmudgeon. With such complexity in mind, this chapter turns now to discuss some of the established but mostly *perceived* health effects of humor and laughter.

PHYSIOLOGICAL AND PSYCHOLOGICAL HEALTH EFFECTS

Humor was associated with physical health in ancient times when it was believed that people were constituted of four bodily fluids –known as the four humors. The four fluids that made up these humors were thought to be phlegm; yellow bile; black bile; and blood. It was believed that in each different person, one of the humors predominated in their body and this was the foundation of their disposition to life. If one had an excess of yellow bile then one was *choleric* which caused mostly irritability and anger; an excess of black bile created a *melancholic* disposition which caused gloominess; a person was apathetic and sluggish when an excess of phlegm was perceived (*phlegmatic* disposition) while the *sanguine* person was thought to be cheerful as a result of having sufficient blood. It was believed that if one could achieve a harmonious combination of the four humors then good health ensued (Arikha, 2008; Clark & Watson, 2008; Plester, 2015a). Traditional medical practices were based on the *four humors* theory for roughly 2500 years (Arikha, 2008). From these physiological origins, humor morphed from describing a perceived balance of fluids to describing a state of mind or disposition and furthermore became linked to responses arising from funny remarks and occurrences (McGhee, 1979). Therefore humor combines a physiological response such as laughter or smiling with a psychological component such as cognitive appreciation of joking or a funny event. It is this complex reaction between body and mind, also incorporating emotive responses, that makes humor difficult to understand and analyze. After all, the same joke may result in a group laughing uproariously, mere smiles from some people, tight grimaces from others, a complete non-response in some cases (also called *unlaughter* see Butler, 2015) and even open condemnation from offended others.

Laughter is often considered to be a positive emotion in itself when it should be perhaps considered an external reflection of a (usually) positive emotion. It is usual to consider someone who is laughing to be in a positive emotional state and one might assume that the person laughing is experiencing joy, happiness, merriment, mirth or the like. The pleasure experience in laughter has been compared to sexual orgasm and the dopaminergic rewards associated with hedonic sensations (Carbelo & Jáuregui, 2006). Humor is most commonly perceived as delightful and pleasure is created through the physical expression of emotion (Martin, 2007). Psychological humor theorists (such as Rod Martin and Sigmund Freud) argue that the ability to express and release strong compulsions such as sexuality and aggression through humor, is both pleasurable and cathartic. In fact, humor offers an acceptable outlet for these sensations which otherwise often must be repressed in the concerns for socially appropriate behavior and good taste.

However, the phenomenon of laughter does not always happy and pleasurable emotions (often assumed) and can instead, sometimes be an expression of embarrassment, confusion, unkind mocking or even cruelty. Laughter can be hostile and aggressive or can be expressed at matters that other people find tragic, sacred or highly serious and thus can invoke distress, offence and discord (Carbelo & Jáuregui, 2006). Billig (2005) argues that it this aspect of humor, the ability for it to be mocking, deriding and highly offensive, that is under-researched and ignored in society as it is much more popular to focus on the positive aspects of humor and the more positive emotions that are invoked when humor is warm, inclusive and experienced as funny and enjoyable.

A signature strength of human beings is that of having a sense of humor which is attributed to physical, psychological and social advantages (Carbelo & Jáuregui, 2006). Psychological benefits include experiences of joy, satisfaction, well-being, stress reduction and prevention of depression while physical advantages pertain to a higher tolerance of pain, improved immunity functions and enhanced cardio-vascular health (Carbelo & Jáuregui, 2006). A sense of humor may help suffering people promote a good mood which can help them to get through illness and may even assist in preventing depression (Carbelo & Jáuregui, 2006). Many studies have demonstrated that humor can raise a person's tolerance to pain (Zweyer, Velker & Ruch, 2004) as well as contribute to a 'subjective perception of better health, which is no small matter' (Carbelo & Jáuregui, 2006: 22).

Wijewardena, Härtel and Samaratunge (2010) argue that a key healthful benefit of humor is gained through using humor to fortify people's psychological resilience. In this workplace study resilience is seen to reduce work stress and burnout and such a reduction is both desirable and healthy. Humor can be seen as an 'emotion-focused coping strategy' (Wijewardena et al., 2010: 264) that allows bottled up emotions to be released, which offers a healthy respite from tension. Wijewardena and colleagues claim that the appraisal of humor is important to how people react to it- that is, if humor is perceived as constructive then positive emotional reactions will ensue with the reverse situation being that seemingly destructive humor will more than likely create negative emotional reactions.

Although some humor can be perceived as mocking and this may be considered destructive, one of the oldest humor theories (*superiority theory*) posits that we laugh at others out of a sense of superiority or one-up-man-ship (Bergson, 1911; Douglas, 1999; Freud, 1905; Gruner, 1997; Hobbes, 1640). The superiority theories can be dated back as far as Plato and Aristotle (in Martin, 2007) and these ancient philosophers argued that laughter arises from nastiness and takes pleasure in the misfortune of others. Hobbes (1640) extended this notion and suggested that people laugh at adversity, folly or gaucheness because in that moment, they themselves are not unfortunate, clumsy or stupid and so people feel superior to the hapless victim who is laughable. Hobbes describes this thus:

> Men laugh at mischances and indecencies wherein there lieth no wit nor jest at all...also men laugh at the *infirmities* of others, by comparison wherewith their own abilities are set off and illustrated...for what is else the recommending of ourselves to our own good opinion, by comparison with another man's infirmity or absurdity?. (Hobbes, 1640: 45 emphasis in original)

Superiority theories of humor suggest that people deal with the unpleasant aspects of life through humor and that they reduce a threatening or harmful situation by making it funny (Wijewardena et al., 2010). Thus humor helps people manage their emotions which is perceived to be good for their health. The idea that humor and laughter offer health benefits is a popular one in the 21st century (Martin, 2007) but this idea has been 'touted for centuries' (Martin, 2007: 309). Some of the bodily substances believed to be beneficially affected by humor are endorphins, cytokines (small protein cells that affect the behavior of other cells) and immunoglobulins. Health is seen as an interaction between psychological, social, biological and cultural factors and humor falls into the realm of health psychology concerned with how 'behavior, cognitions, and emotions can influence health, wellness and illness' (Martin, 2007: 309). In summarizing many of the studies and perceived benefits of humor upon health, Martin concludes that the most consistent research support concerns the analgesic effects of laughter, that is, people can tolerate greater levels of pain when experiencing humor. Martin also summarizes that the research on humor's influence on immunity is inconclusive but he does concede that humorous people may enjoy a greater quality of life because a good sense of humor helps them cope with stress. Although Martin asserts that the causal relationship between good humor and good health is yet to be proven, he does acknowledge that there is no harm in encouraging people to enjoy humor which may make life more enjoyable and Martin calls for further systematic research into humor-health connections. Furthermore, in accord with Wijewardena and colleagues (2010) he suggests that investigating humor styles may be important as it is likely that different effects are generated by hostile, dark or biting humor than by benign forms of humor. Therefore this is an ambiguous, fragmented area and worthy of more sustained and systematic research as intuitively, and through the early limited research, it feels that humor and health effects are interlinked, scholars just need to investigate how, when, where and why.

SOCIAL INTERACTIONS

This chapter has discussed humor that helps people manage emotions, humor that creates emotions itself and some of the ambiguous health effects, and the uniting aspect to all of these sections is the interactive nature of humor. Humor is an interaction and usually a social interaction. Most humor occurs *between* people and most people laugh with others significantly more than when they are alone (Martin, 2007). Humor is ubiquitous and occurs in all cultures and is an important part of human interactions although it can be considered a 'peculiar combination of friendliness and antagonism' (Radcliffe-Brown, 1940, p. 196).

When looking at humor from a functional position, one of the key attributes of humor is the ability to develop and maintain solidarity among those sharing the humor (Holmes, 2000). Humor can establish and delineate group memberships including family groups, friendship circles and workplace groups (Everts, 2003; Lampert & Ervin –Tripp 2006; Romero & Pescosolido, 2008). Groups develop their own patterns and norms for humor and part of group membership involves appropriate responses to humor, using humor appropriately and observing socially constructed boundaries of humor (Plester, 2009; Schnurr & Plester, 2016). For example, teasing among those in a friendship group made up of people from different socio-cultural backgrounds, also serves as a way to strengthen group bonds and foster solidarity (Habib, 2008). Everts (2003) found that in family groups even mocking and seemingly aggressive humor can create relational harmony and intimacy. So it is commonly agreed that humor can be viewed as a functional device that can help groups of people in social situations become closer, more integrated with shared camaraderie. However humor is a tricky 'device' because the absolute opposite can, and does, occur. A seemingly warm, well-intentioned joke can backfire horribly and cause distress and chaos. This can occur through ignorance or misjudgment although it can also be intentional and planned. A key point is that humor is highly contextual and a joke that goes down well with a group of friends in the pub may not be readily accepted in a workplace context or a community meeting for example.

In social behavior, humor can be a key factor in defining who is an integrated member of a group (the in-group) and who is excluded and therefore part of the out-group. Social Identity Theory (SIT) suggests that identification with, and participation in, groups is an important part of people's social identity (Tajfel, 1978) and being a member of a specific group can be important and highly valued by different people. Group dynamics can be complicated but research suggests that the social interaction of shared laughter can both create and strengthen group identity (Terrion & Ashforth, 2002). As a group develops, it generates its' own distinctive joking culture and socialised group members understand the humorous references or 'in-jokes' which they build upon to produce further humorous interaction (Fine & De Soucey, 2005). Integrated groups construct norms and boundaries to unify their group culture (Kahn, 1989) and in order to fully become one of the group, a newcomer must, over time, understand the group's social behavior and boundaries to humor and joking (see Plester, 2009).

In formally created groups, humor can help people to 'break the ice' and can relieve tension and awkwardness that may be present in the early stages of group development. Over time the humor will develop and change and the group collects their own repertoire of jokes and humor references that relate to their group activities and interactions (Plester, 2015; Terrion & Ashforth, 2002). A newcomer needs to work out the existing humor patterns in order to socialise into the group and become fully accepted. Joking repertories are one of the strongest indicators of group membership and inclusion. Humor is a social lubricant that enhances effectiveness, cohesiveness, communication and creativity and the positive affect created by humor enhances social processes (Romero, 2005; Romero & Pescosolido, 2008). However, it is again notable that research into social and group processes does heavily emphasize positive affect and the problematic 'dark' effects of destructive, offensive humor are less researched and investigated. Thus my final example illustrates a workplace team where humor that had been universally enjoyed within the group became the basis for discord and created ill-will and disharmony.

Brenda* entered an Information Technology (IT) organization as a newcomer to an established and successfully performing phone-sales team. The senior manager was impressed with her technological capabilities and she was a mature employee, in her late forties. The team she joined was comprised of mostly younger people in their twenties, and team members all worked in an open-plan office space. On her second day in the team Brenda overheard Cathy, who was situated in adjoining cubicle, talking and laughing with a long-term customer. Through her laughter Cathy loudly joked '*oh you're just being a wanker today!*' (In Plester, 2015). After Cathy hung up the phone, Brenda approached her and firmly reprimanded the younger woman declaring that it was wrong to use profane language with customers. Cathy was extremely offended and outraged by this admonishment, feeling that as a newcomer, Brenda had no rights to comment on her behavior.

This interchange was the beginning of a period of very unhappy group relations. Brenda continued her stern chastisements and reproached her young co-workers for their continuous jocular abuse of each other, and their banter with well-known customers. In retaliation the work group excluded Brenda from all of their social interchanges especially their humor and joking. They interacted with Brenda formally and only in regards to work-related matters. After a month in the company Brenda felt completely isolated and Cathy had requested that she be physically moved to a different workspace - away from Brenda. Senior managers were worried because their successful, cheerful and integrated team had become tense and unhappy. Furthermore, Brenda was unable to integrate and become part of her work group. After trying different options, moving people around, team activities and the like, the team manager took drastic action. He decided not to renew Brenda's contract and she departed from the company. Brenda left the company reluctantly and in a final discussion, she admitted that her colleagues had good values but that she had misjudged them based on some of their humor.

In this sad example all of the protagonists were effectively performing their workplace tasks and activities but the disagreement in humor styles and appropriateness of group humor caused an insurmountable rift in the group relations. On the one hand, Brenda was disgusted by the tone, style and profanity in the group's humor and on the other hand, the group members were affronted by Brenda's criticism of their group norms in regards to humor. The negative emotions caused by the disparities in humor acceptance were strong enough to dismember the team and cause the loss of a treasured job. This example demonstrates the importance of humor in social interaction and the power of humor to create strong emotion. It also illustrates the significance of socializing into a group carefully while norms and values are assimilated and highlights that humor patterns are a key aspect of group solidarity and group relations.

CONCLUSION

Humor both causes and mitigates emotions and all of the extensive list of emotions may play out in humor interactions. It is common for humor to be perceived as linking to positive and pleasurable emotions such as joy, mirth, happiness and enthusiasm. This chapter has argued that although humor can and does commonly create positive feelings, humor is also firmly linked to negative emotions such as disgust, anger, and sadness and humor can be destructive and hurtful. A significant human emotion is embarrassment and many people attempt to avoid this emotion at all costs but some forms of humor mock, deride and create emotions of embarrassment and humiliation as some of the cited examples attest. A seminal section of the chapter discussed the idea that humor allows a relief and release of emotion through being able to express ideas that must usually be repressed and constrained. Humor can be a form of social liberation whereby the spirit and one's genuine impulses may momentarily fly free and be honest but this still carries a significant risk of upsetting others. The contextual elements of humor were emphasized and are highly significant. A joke enjoyed with friends over a glass of wine may be totally inappropriate in a different context and people learn to astutely judge when and where humor works and which types fit which situation.

Sadly, humor does go wrong sometimes and causes great upset and even, as discussed in the chapter, actual tragedy. It may be that when humor is used and it doesn't work, this heightens the emotions that are experienced and people then express extreme indignation and outrage at perceived transgressions of humor and with humor. On the other hand, a large amount of humor that could cause upset and dissension simply flies under the radar, is accepted and never challenged and the joker gets away with some risky ideas. This is the heart of humor- the complexity, the ambiguity, the risk and the never quite knowing if it will fail or create hilarity. Humor is important but underestimated and under-researched. There might be some health benefits but there might be some strong detriments that we haven't worked out yet. It's why we love it and hate it –both strong emotive terms, but humor is an emotive issue and one that we should embrace enthusiastically, warily, happily and sadly- all at once.

*Pseudonyms are used throughout.

REFERENCES

Alexander, D. & Wells, W. (1991). Reactions of police officers to body-handling after a major disaster: A before and after comparison. *British Journal of Psychiatry, 159*: 547-555.

Arikha, N. (2008). Just life in a nutshell: Humours as common sense. *The philosophical forum, 39*(3), 303-314.

Ashkanasy, N.M., Härtel, C.E.J. & Zerbe, W.J. (2000). *Emotions in the workplace: research, theory and practice.* Quorum: Westport.

Astedt-Kurki, P., Isola, A., Tammentie, T., & Kervinen, U. 2001. Importance of humor to client–nurse relationships and clients' well-being. *International Journal of Nursing Practice, 7*(2), 119–125.

Ashforth, B.E. and Humphrey, R.H., (1995). Emotion in the workplace: a reappraisal. Human Relations 48, pp. 97–125.

Attardo, S. (1997). The semantic foundations of cognitive theories of humor. *Humor, International Journal of Humor Research 4*(10), 293 -347.

BBC News. (2012). *Duchess of Cambridge hoax call nurse found dead.* http://www.bbc.com/news/uk-20645838, 7 Dec 2012.

BBC News. (2014). Royal hoax DJ Mel Greig 'was sent bullets in the post' http://www.bbc.com/news/uk-29602623, 13 Oct 2014.

Bergson, H. (1911). *Laughter. An essay on the meaning of the comic.* (C. Brereton & F. Rothwell, Trans. 1935 ed.). London: MacMillan & Co.

Billig, M. (2005). *Laughter and ridicule. Towards a social critique of humour.* London: Sage.

Bolton, S. & Boyd, C. (2003). "Trolley dolly or skilled emotion manager? Moving on from Hochschild's 'emotional labour,' " *Work, Employment and Society, 17*(2), 289-308.

Bowers, R., & Smith, P. S. (2004). Wit, humor and Elizabethan coping. *Humor. International Journal of Humor Research, 17*(3), 181-218.

Carbelo, B. & Jáuregui, E. (2006). Positive emotions: Positive humor. *Papeles del Psicólogo, 27*(1), 18-30.

Chapman, A. J., & Foot, H. C. (Eds.). (1976). *Humour and laughter: Theory, research and applications.* London: John Wiley & Sons.

Clark, L.A. & Watson, D. (2008). Temperament: An organizing paradigm for trait psychology. In Oliver, J.P., Robins, R.W., Pervin, L. A. (Eds.). *Handbook of personality: Theory and Research* (3rd ed) pp. 265-286. New York, NY US: Guilford PressCooper, C. (2005). Just joking around? *Employee humor expression as an ingratiatory behaviour. The Academy of Management Review, 30*(4), 765-776.

Cooper, C. (2008). Elucidating the bonds of workplace humor: A relational process model. *Human Relations, 61*(8), 1087-1115.

Dean, R.A. & Major, J.E. (2008). From critical care to comfort care: the sustaining value of humor. *International Journal of Nursing Practice, 17*(8), 1088–11095.

Douglas, M. (1999). *Implicit meanings. Selected essays in Anthropology.* (2nd ed.). London: Routledge.

Downe, P. (1999). Laughing when it hurts: Humor and violence in the lives of Costa Rican prostitutes. *Women's Studies International Forum 22*: 63-78.

Duncan, J. W., Smeltzer, L. R., & Leap, T. L. (1990). Humor and Work: Applications of joking behaviour to management. *Journal of Management, 16*(2), 255-279.

Ekman, P. (1992) An argument for basic emotions, Cognition and Emotion, 6:3-4, 169-200.

Everts, E. (2003). Identifying a particular family humor style: A sociolinguistic discourse analysis. *Humor, 16*(4), 369-412.

Fine, G. A., & De Soucey, M. (2005). Joking Cultures: Humor Themes as Social Regulation in Group Life. *Humor. International Journal of Humor Research, 18*(1), 122.

Freud, S. (1905). *Jokes and their relations to the unconscious.* (A. Richards, Trans. 1991). London: Penguin.

Freud, S. (1927). Humor. *International Journal of Psychoanalysis, 9*, 1-6.

Fry, W. F. J., & Allen, M. (1976). Humour as a creative experience: The development of a Hollywood humorist. In A. J. Chapman & H. C. Foot (Eds.), *Humour and laughter: Theory, research and applications*, 245-258. London: John Wiley & Sons.

Godkewitsch, M. (1976). Physiological and verbal indices of arousal in rated humour. In A. J. Chapman & H. C. Foot (Eds.), *Humour and laughter: Theory, research and applications*, (pp. 117-138). London: John Wiley & Sons.

Gruner, C. R. (1997). *The game of humor. A Comprehensive theory of why we laugh.* New Brunswick: Transaction Publishers.

Habib, R. (2008). Humor and disagreement: Identity construction and cross-cultural enrichment. *Journal of Pragmatics* 40: 1117–1145.

Hobbes, T. (1640). Hobbes tripos in three discourses: Human nature. In W. S. Molesworth (Ed.), *The English works of Thomas Hobbes of Malmesbury. Vol. IV.* 183-945. London: John Bohn.

Holmes, J. (2000). Politeness, power and provocation: How humour functions in the workplace. *Discourse studies, 2*(2), 159-185.

Josefowtz, N. & Gadon, H. (1989). Hazing: Uncovering one of the best-kept secrets of the workplace. Business horizons, 32(3), 22-26.

Kahn, W. (1989). Toward a sense of organisational humor: Implications for organisational diagnosis and change. *The Journal of Applied Behavioral Science, 25*(1), 45-63.

Karl, K. & Peluchette, J. (2006). Does Workplace Fun Buffer the Impact of Emotional Exhaustion on Job Dissatisfaction?: A Study of Health Care Workers, *Journal of Behavioral and Applied Management*: 7 (2): 128-141.

Karl, K. (2006). Does workplace fun buffer the impact of emotional exhaustion on job dissatisfaction?: A study of health care workers. *Journal of Behavioral and Applied Management, 7*(2), 128-142.

Koestler, A. (1964). *The act of creation.* London: Hutchinson & Co.

Lampert, M.D. & Ervin- Tripp, S.M. (2006). Risky laughter: Teasing and self-directed joking among male and female friends. *Journal of Pragmatics, 38*, 51-72.

Lively, K.J. (2006). *Emotions.* New York: Oxford Unity Press.

Martin, R. A. (2007). *The psychology of humor. An integrative approach.* Burlington, MA: Elsevier.

Mc Ghee, P. E. (1979). *Humor. Its origin and development.* San Francisco: Freeman and Co.

Moran, C. & Massam, M. (1997). An evaluation of humor in emergency work. *The Australian and New Zealand Journal of Disaster and Trauma, 3*: 1-11.

Morreall, J. (1983). *Taking laughter seriously.* Albany, NY: State University of New York.

Obrdlik, M. (1941). Gallows humor. *American Sociological Review, 47*: 709-713.

Plester, B.A. (2009). Crossing the line: Boundaries of workplace humour and fun. *Employee Relations, 31*(6), 584-599.

Plester, B. A (2015a). *The complexity of workplace humour: Laughter, jokers and the dark side.* Dordrecht: Springer.

Plester, B. A. (2015b). Take it like a man! Performing hegemonic masculinity through organizational humour. *ephemera, 15*(3), 537-559.

Radcliffe-Brown, A. R. (1940). On joking relationships. *Africa: Journal of the International African Institute, 13*(3), 195-210.

Romero, E. J. (2005). The effect of humor on mental state and work effort. *Work, organization and emotion, 1*(2), 137-149.

Romero, E.J. & Pescosolido, A. (2008). Humor and group effectiveness. *Human Relations, 61*(3), 395-418.

Samson, A. C. & Gross, J. J. (2012). Humor as emotion regulation: The differential consequences of negative versus positive humor. *Cognition and emotion, 26*(2), 375-384.

Sanders, T. (2004). Controllable laughter: Managing sex work through humor. *Sociology, 38*(2): 273-291.

Schnurr, S. & Plester, B. A. (2016). Functionalist discourse analysis of humor. In Attardo, Salvatore (Ed.) *Routledge Handbook of Language and Humor.* Routledge.

Smith, M (2009). *The art of the practical joke.* Paper presented at the American Folklore Society, Idaho, Oct 2009.

Tajfel, H. (1978). *Differentiation between social groups: Studies in the social psychology of intergroup relations.* London: Academic Press.

Terrion, J. L., & Ashforth, B. E. (2002). From 'I' to 'we': The role of putdown humor and identity in the development of a temporary group. *Human Relations, 55*(1), 55-87.

Weick, K. E. & Westley, F. (1996). Organisational learning: Affirming an oxymoron. In S. R. Clegg, C. Hardy & W. R. Nord (Eds.), *Handbook of organisation studies*, (pp.440-58). London: Sage.

Weisfeld, G.E. (2006). Humor appreciation as an adaptive esthetic emotion. *Humor. International Journal of Humor Research, 19*(1), p1-26.

Wijewardena, N., Härtel, C.E.J., & Samaratunge, R. (2010). A laugh a day is sure to keep the blues away: managers use of humor and the construction and destruction of employees resistance. *Emotions and Organizational Dynamism.* Published online: 08 March 2015; 259-278. http://dx.doi.org/10.1108/S1746-9791(2010)0000006014.

Wilson, C. P. (1979). *Jokes. Form, content, use and function.* London: Academic Press.

Zweyer, K., Velker, B., & Ruch, W. (2004). Do cheerfulness, exhilaration, and humor production moderate pain tolerance? A FACS study. *Humor, 17*(1-2), 85-121.

BIOGRAPHICAL SKETCH

Dr Barbara Plester

Barbara is currently Senior Lecturer in the Department of Management and International Business. Barbara joined the University of Auckland Business School in 2007 and completed her PhD in management at Massey University, Albany campus in 2008. Her current research explores: workplace humor; fun; flow and engagement; transgression; virtual team communication; social media impacts at work; and her most recent project investigates food rituals in organizations. Barbara is the University of Auckland's academic representative for the Human Resources Institute of New Zealand (HRINZ). Prior to her academic career, Barbara worked in Publishing and Information Technology companies and has practical experience in Sales, Marketing and HRM.

As part of the Organization Studies group in MIB and Barbara teaches papers on communication, organizational behaviour and HRM. Currently she is the director of the Masters programme and Graduate Advisor for prospective postgraduate students. Barbara is a member of the Peer Review team committed to continuous teaching improvement in the Business School. She a member of: International Society of Humor Scholars (ISHS); Australian-New Zealand Academy of Management (ANZAM), European Group of Organizational Studies (EGOS) and Standing Conference on Organizational Symbolism (SCOS).

In: Humor
Editor: Holly Phillips
ISBN: 978-1-63484-787-2
© 2016 Nova Science Publishers, Inc.

Chapter 6

OSTENSIBLY INAPPROPRIATE HUMOUR: A CASE STUDY OF AN EMOTIONAL RUPTURE

Peter Branney[1], PhD, and Karl Witty[2], MA
[1]Senior Lecturer in Social Psychology,
School of Social, Psychological and Communication Sciences,
Leeds Beckett University, Leeds, UK
[2]Team Lead for CommUNIty Partnerships,
Institute for Health and Wellbeing, Leeds Beckett University, Leeds, UK

ABSTRACT

Aim: To explore areas of healthcare where the deployment of humour or response to patient-initiated humour and/or laughter by a health profession would be considered inappropriate by their peers and/or their patient and/or the patients' family and friends.

Background: Functionalist, relief and incongruity theories attempt to explain humour but there is a dearth of empirical evidence in healthcare. This is particularly so in relation to penile cancer where research shows that humour is present, and while patients value it in healthcare interaction they nevertheless fear ridicule.

Method: A case design, via secondary analysis, was employed. The case was selected from the Patients Experiences of Penile Cancer study for three reasons; first, the interview contained humour, second, the researchers felt it would have been inappropriate for them to use humour and, third, the interviewee broke down crying.

Findings: Biographical disclosure was difficult, some chuckling emerged as a release about something uncomfortable and there was an emotional rupture that exceeded the interview, leading to a break.

Conclusion: This case study extends our understanding of humour in healthcare by illustrating an emotional rupture in an encounter where the interviewee is struggling to respond, saying little in response to questions and probes for discussion. While humour can be used to build rapport, the implication of this study is that it should be avoided interaction is difficult.

INTRODUCTION

This chapter is concerned with areas of healthcare that are ostensibly too sensitive for humour. As McCreaddie and Wiggin's point out, there is a great deal of opinion about humour in health care but little empirical research (McCreaddie & Wiggins, 2008). While arguably based on a great deal of professional experience, these opinions raise questions worth consideration. What is it, for example, for humour to be inappropriate? What happens, in settings where humour is ostensibly inappropriate, when patients initiate humour and/or laughter emerges? Consequently, we want to use this chapter to explore areas of healthcare that are 'no-go' for humour. That is, where the deployment of humour or response to patient-initiated humour and/or laughter by a health profession would be considered inappropriate by their peers and, importantly, their patient and/or the patients' family and friends. We shall use Gough's (2004) term of *emotional rupture* to help us define 'inappropriate' as a breach in a particular interaction between a healthcare professional and patient and/or patients' family. That is, an emotional response, such as anger or crying, that exceeds the interaction in question and changes the relationship between those involved.

Services for the diagnosis and treatment of penile cancer arguably exemplify those areas of care considered by some (see Hunt, 1993) to be inappropriate for the use of humour. The standard of care in the treatment of penile cancer is surgical excision of the primary tumour and a two-centimetre margin of healthy tissue (Minhas et al., 2005). While 80% survive for at least five years (Pizzocaro et al., 2010), those receiving the diagnosis must live with the consequences of treatment. Research both challenges and supports the argument that humour is inappropriate in penile cancer services. Men diagnosed with penile cancer do report, at times, welcoming the use of humour in their care (Witty et al., 2013) and that it helps build rapport with health professionals (Branney et al., 2014) although they did fear ridicule (idib.) because of their diagnosis and treatment. Importantly, this research highlights the complexity of humour and that it is present in the care of penile cancer. We argue therefore that penile cancer services provide an ideal context for the study of ostensibly inappropriate humour.

Notwithstanding calls for the inclusion of patients' experiences in research about urological cancers (Branney, White, Jain, Hiley, & Flowers, 2009), case studies offer an exploration in detail of an individual's journey while retaining a sense of the wider context. As Yin (2009) highlights, case studies are particularly useful when there is little understanding of the boundaries between the phenomenon and context in question. This means that we can use a case study to explore a patient's unique experiences of penile cancer care while allowing that they are affected directly and indirectly by wider conditions that, for example, potentially make humour inappropriate. As Branney et al., argue (Branney, Witty, Bagnall, South, & White, 2012), a patient is like an employee "who has agency within their role, which is defined by their employing organization and wider cultural, historical, and social values" (p. 866).

Before introducing the case study, we shall explore how functional, relief, incongruity theories of humour relate to healthcare, particularly in relation to situations that may be too sensitive. Additionally, we shall outline the integration-interpersonal approach to humour theories in healthcare and a three-part conceptualization of intersubjectivity.

Theories of Humour

Incongruity theory conceptualizes what it is about a specific joke or pun that make it funny (Billig, 2005; Giora, 1991). Focusing on the cognitive aspects of a joke, humour is achieved through an incongruity between the ideas in the joke. Billig gives an example that invokes an incongruity between alternative meanings of the word 'tank': there are two fish in a tank and one turns to the other and says, 'Do you know how to drive this?' (Billig, 2005). Extending beyond the semantics of words, the theory encompasses potential incongruities between behaviour and social norms explaining why our actions may, regardless of our intent, be met with laughter. Like an evolution of social standards, Shaftsbury argues that behavior is subject to the 'test of ridicule' (Shaftsbury, 1999(1711)); actions met with laughter are identified as inappropriate and should therefore be avoided or discarded. Humour can therefore signal that behavior or the topic of discussion is in some way incongruous with what is expected, which explains why humour can be a vehicle for the non-threatening voicing of complaints (Du Pré, 1998). There is one rare example, within a wider study, that illustrates the double occurrence of incongruity. A man diagnosed and treated for prostate cancer reported that a doctor's 'happy go lucky' way of discussing his feminisation through hormone therapy was insensitive (Chapple & Ziebland, 2002). The doctor is arguably drawing upon and therefore reinforcing notions of what is to be a man by highlighting an incongruity between such norms and his patient. Nevertheless, his patients' account of how he felt about this interaction signals an incongruity between what is expected of a medical encounter and the behavior of the doctor. Incongruity theory fails to differentiate between raillery and ridicule or light-hearted and contemptuous humour. The intention may be to initiate friendly banter but may be experienced as ridicule, which highlights the importance of context, relations between those involved and the interpretation of meaning. Discerning an acceptable balance of humour relies on social norms and the experiences of speaker, audience and subject and unfortunately, the theory is difficult to tease apart and apply to health care interactions. This might explain why there is little in health care that relates to incongruity theory.

Rather than being a discrete joke or pun, functionalist theory (Billig, 2005) conceptualizes humour as part of social interaction. Through interaction, humour builds up and breaks out. Laughter can, for example, show that the particular interaction is being experienced as enjoyable (Bergson, 2008(1900)). Research shows that humour can confer a positive emotional state, adding to the interpersonal relations between those involved (Francis, Monahan, & Berger, 1999) and smoothing the flow of conversation (Norrick, 1993). This means that humour can be a vehicle for non-comedic meaning (Mulkay, 1988), such as patients voicing complaints in a non-threatening manner (Du Pré 1998). Health care professionals can use humour to build rapport, demonstrate empathy and quickly communicate persuasive messages while dealing with the mortality of the body (Du Pré, 1998). In particular, patients report that humour is comforting because it allows them to speak openly about their health in a 'laid-back and friendly' environment (Smith, Braunack-Mayer, Wittert, & Warin, 2008). Additionally, patients report that sharing humour with their health care professional makes them feel 'normal,' reducing the power imbalance so that the patient can discuss their vulnerabilities (Oliffe & Thorne, 2007).

Combining ideas about the physiological release of nervous energy (Bain, 1859; Billig, 2005) and Freud's notion of tendentious jokes as expressing something socially censored (Freud, 2001(1905)), relief theory could be seen as release of tension about the socially taboo. A dirty, sexist or racist joke, for example, is never 'just a joke' but a way of breaking social conventions and saying something that is proscribed. It is no surprise, for example, that Legman's analysis of sexual humour is in two volumes and over 2,000 pages. In contrast to notion of laughter as signaling enjoyment, relief theory suggests that it may be evidence of, and a technique for managing, tension. Consequently, humour is a mechanism for managing tension, through which we can evade embarrassment (Goffman, 1967) and/or taking a problem (too) seriously (Kelly & Dickinson, 1997). Humour can dissipate emotion by signalling a time-out from an anxiety-provoking situation, which could be particularly useful in health care settings (Smith et al., 2008). Patients report ill-health makes them feel vulnerable in front of health professionals and humour is one way of dealing with their vulnerability (Smith et al., 2008). From this theoretical perspective and given the focus on pathology, bodily decline and mortality in health care, it is little surprise that humour is found in approximately 85% of nursing interactions (Adamle & Ludwick, 2005). Indeed, there is evidence that suggests humour confers health benefits on those that use it, such as nursing educators who have have lower emotional exhaustion and higher levels of personal accomplishment than those who do not (Talbot & Lunden, 2000).

Integration-Interpersonal Approach

There is an approach that integrates incongruity, functionalist and relief theories in health care settings (Branney et al., 2015). The potential for comedy and ridicule lies in incongruities between social norms and a patients' experiences and abilities as a consequence of their illness and or treatment. Additionally, the emotions patients' experience can be contained (functionalist) and released (relief) through humorous interaction. This integration of theories places, for the health professional, an emphasis on interpersonal skills (hence, the integration-interpersonal approach) and both supports and contradicts notions of no-go areas for humour in health care, which we shall explain with reference to intersubjectivity.

Revising Lacan's tripartite structure for what he calls logical time (the instant of seeing, the time for understanding and the moment of concluding; 2006[1945]), it helps to think of three moments of intersubjectivity; i) seeing, responding to the ii) other and responding to the iii) other's response to you.

Seeing is an observation of the world and in this context is an assessment of whether humour is appropriate or not. While it is the first moment of intersubjectivity, seeing has no sense of another subjective being. As such, seeing is akin to opinions about no-go areas for humour and incongruity theory holds a key to such assessments. Health professionals can ask if their patients' experiences and/or abilities as a consequence of their condition are in some way incongruous with social norms. While this means that there is the potential for humour, there is a risk that it may be experienced as ridicule. Branney et al.'s (Branney et al., 2014) advice that health care professionals working with men diagnosed for penile cancer might want to avoid humour until after treatment is akin to seeing for its reading of situations with no reference to the specific person encountered. The second moment of intersubjectivity is where we first encounter the other and therefore consider how to respond to them. Are they, for example, like Barry who reports that he is 'nobbler' that persistently jokes and likes the 'banter' with the penile cancer specialists because it puts him at ease (ibid.)? Or are they like Norman, who thinks that humour is an inappropriate topic when talking about his experiences of penile cancer (ibid.)? Indeed, Barry illustrates that regardless of whether a health care professional intends to avoid humour in what they consider to be a 'no-go' situation, patients may initiate humour and/or laugh. Consequently, a health care professional will need to draw upon their interpersonal skills in considering how to respond to their patient, potentially containing or releasing emotions. Last, actions within an interaction will inevitably lead to a response, which leads us the moment of intersubjectivity when the subject responds to the response of the other to them. From both a functional and relief perspective, humour occurs over time, even if it may appear to erupt or break through at specific points. This opens up the possibility for interactional repair when a patient's response indicates that they consider the health care professional's actions inappropriate.

The integration-interpersonal approach gives us some guidance about the application of humour theories in healthcare settings. Importantly, this approach allows us to value opinions about 'no-go' areas for humour for their reading of a situation when we know nothing about the person or people to be encountered. Indeed, such opinions are arguably based on experience where health professionals have learned, from the response of their patients, that their attempts to use humour have been inappropriate. Furthermore, this approach orientates us towards the patient encountered; that is, to the 'other' who potentially signals that humour is appropriate or inappropriate. In particular, what is it for humour to be inappropriate and what happens when humour and/or laughter emerges in such situations?

AIM

Consequently, the aim of this chapter is to use a case study to explore areas of healthcare where the deployment of humour or response to patient-initiated humour and/or laughter by a health profession would be considered inappropriate by their peers and/or their patient and/or the patients' family and friends. The case study will be of a man who has been diagnosed and treated for penile cancer because it is an area of healthcare where humour is ostensibly inappropriate but research nevertheless shows that it is present, and patients' value it, even if they fear ridicule (Branney et al., 2014). The case study is taken from an interview for Patients' Experiences of Penile Cancer (Branney et al., 2013; Branney et al., 2015; Branney, Witty, & Eardley, 2011; Witty et al., 2014; Witty et al., 2013), where the researchers felt strongly that humour was inappropriate.

METHOD

The Wider PEPC Study

The aim of Patients' Experiences of Penile Cancer (Branney et al., 2011) was to explore the experiences of those diagnosed and treated for penile cancer and publish them on the award winning healthtalk.org (previously called healthtalkonline.org and, before that, the database of patients' experiences or DIPEx; Herxheimer et al., 2000). Following the interview, the interviewer wrote a biography summarizing the participant's journey with penile cancer, which each participant checked, making corrections as necessary and adding further details for clarification. While humour emerged in the interviews, it nevertheless felt to the researchers that in some of the interviews it would have been inappropriate for them to initiate and/or respond in a humorous manner. Consequently, the PEPC interviews provide a unique opportunity to explore humour in an area of healthcare where it is ostensibly inappropriate.

Design

A case study design, via secondary analysis, was employed because it allowed us to explore humour when the boundaries between the phenomenon (the particular experiences of, and those recounted in, the interview) and the context (healthcare for penile cancer) are unclear. As Branney et al., (Branney, Strickland, Darby, White, & Jain, 2016) argue, the sampling rational when researching rare conditions, rather than aiming to seek data saturation, is to work out how best to use the information gathered, given the limitation to recruitment. Consequently, it is important to make best use of the data collected in PEPC before seeking to collect new data. The narrative history design in PEPC, collected through semi-structured interviews, is ideal for a case study via secondary analysis.

Population

Twenty-eight men were recruited from across the UK and interviewed for PEPC, with one withdrawing before publication on healthtalk.org (see Witty for more detail about recruitment). The mean age of participants at interview was 67 years (range = 41-83). Seventeen reported that they were married or in a relationship and twenty-six identified as White and one Asian. The mean age of participants at diagnosis was 63 (range = 41-82) and all had undergone surgery to excise their tumour, ranging from circumcision to total penectomy. At the time of the interview, the mean time since surgery was 3 years (range = 0 to 15 years).

Case Selection

James interview was selected for this case study because it contained three elements. First, James chuckled when talking about some of his experiences and therefore, despite the area of healthcare, humour did emerge. Second, the researchers felt it would have been inappropriate for them to use humour, either in response to James chuckling or at any other time throughout the interview. Despite evidence of laughter, they nevertheless had a subjective response to James that made them feel that in this interaction humour was inappropriate. Last, James started crying and accepted the interviewer's offer to pause the interview. Adopting Gough's (2004) term, *emotional rupture* captures the sense in which James emotions burst through like a crack in a damn that appears small for a brief moment (James pauses in his speech and attempts to hold back sobs) before suddenly and uncontrollably erupting (into crying). Additionally, James crying was an emotional rupture that breached the harmony built up between interviewer (KW) and interviewee up to that point that, despite taking a break, only returned at the interview's resolution. Consequently, a case study should allow us to explore ostensibly inappropriate humour when emotions exceed the interaction in question.

Data Collection

Each interview started with the request, 'please describe your experience of illness, from the point at which you first suspected that there may be something wrong,' inviting participants to position their illness within the wider context of their life. Supplementary questions allowed further insight into issues informed by a participative one-day pilot workshop (Branney et al., 2016). Where participants consented, quotes were published on healthtalk.org as video (N = 13), audio (N = 12) or text (2). The mean interview duration was 66 minutes (ranging from 37 minutes to 2 hours 17 minutes) and James audio-recorded interview lasted 44 minutes, excluding the break, which commenced at 36 minutes. What occurred during the break is what we consider excluded material.

Ethical Considerations

At the time of conducting the interviews, ethical approval for healthtalk studies came from Berkshire Research Ethics Committee (Ref: 12/SC/0495) who are independent of the researchers and have working practices established by the National Health Service (NHS) Patient Safety Agency. In a multi-stage process, consent was negotiated prior to meeting, at the time of the interview (with a signed-consent form) and after the interview had been transcribed and the researcher had written a biography of the participant. In conducting secondary analysis on data about rare conditions, it is important to make the most of the information collected while staying within the bounds of the agreement with the participant. Each participant was sent a copy of their biography and transcript and in a 'future use of interview' form asked to agree to their use in teaching, broadcasting, research and making audio visual resources and other publications.' We explained that their data would form an archive, akin to a genetics databank, which could be shared with researchers as new research questions emerged. The limitation of this future use was that their data would not be used for advertising or purely commercial purposes. Our hope was that the time between interview and seeing the biography and transcript would give participants time to reflect on their involvement before deciding if and how to agree to future use of their data. As well as choosing to use their first name or pseudonym, participants had the choice of allowing us to make their interview available for these purposes as video, audio or transcript only. At the time of the interview, James agreed to audio recording and afterwards consented to the written transcript being available for future use.

Secondary Data Analysis

We would describe this as a theoretically informed inquisitive analysis in which we interrogated the data to build up the case of the emotional rupture. Rather than looking for themes, discourses or a grounded theory our intention was instrumental in taking what Madill and Gough call an 'overarching commitment' (2008) and asking how the case aids our understanding of ostensibly inappropriate humour. After familiarization with the data, a researcher (PB) read through the transcript, coding text and making notes on emotional tone, particular James chuckling and those aspects that suggested humour was inappropriate. Cycling between familiarization and coding, the researcher turned to the biography to help understand James journey with cancer before returning to code the detail of the transcript. Next, the researcher looked across the codes and notes using similarities and differences to chunk them into potential aspects of the case, summarizing quotes and then writing a description of each aspect. Chunking, summarizing and describing was repeated until the researcher felt that they had aspects that each added something unique to our understanding of ostensibly inappropriate humour while combined produced a case that was greater than its constituent parts.

CASE FINDINGS

Aged 67 at the time of interview, James identifies as White British and is married with three adult children. The diagnosis for penile cancer came shortly before his daughter's wedding, and James was anxious that his condition should clash with the event. James works full time in a technical, hands on profession in which he is a sole trader. James has had bowel cancer and it took over two years of medical appointments, treatment with topical cream followed by circumcision before the sore patch on the glans of his penis was diagnosed as cancer. James had been diagnosed a year before the interview and was attending his specialist penile cancer centre every three months for check-ups and has needed no extra medical intervention since treatment.

Difficult, Biographical Disclosure

The way James reveals his story during the interview suggests that the disclosure is difficult for him. Importantly, we want to differentiate between the content of James story and how he tells it. The content – what, when, where and the characters involved – of James story is a difficult one. The two-year and at times painful process towards a diagnosis for penile cancer strikes us, for example, as, at best, indicative of the difficulties faced by people with rare conditions and, at work, an indictment of his health services. Additionally, being diagnosed shortly before the wedding of his daughter highlights James mortality, and what he could miss and those who could be affected by his death. We only understand James story retrospectively and as Parker explains, "the appearance of trauma is something that is constituted after the event as an attempt to give sense to an event that could not be comprehended by the subject" (p. 170). After 13 minutes, for example, we learn that James was diagnosed for bowel cancer. Yet after 32 minutes we learn that the treatment for bowel cancer left him impotent, which means that the risks faced by surgery for penile cancer are potentially less salient. Consequently, there is something else, other than the content of the story, that tells us humour was inappropriate.

When James talks, there are lots of pauses, sometimes even audible sighs, and he appears to have great difficulty remember his experiences of diagnosis, treatment and recovery. As researchers, our interpretations of the pauses and sighs are that James was thinking about his answer. Rather than, for example, indicating frustration, our interpretation from the interview is that the long sigh in Extract 1 is James taking his time to think about his answer to the question. In Extract 2, this difficulty of recall is palpable as pauses, err and erms show James struggling to remember receiving his diagnosis.

Extract 1

Interview: So what do you think did cause you to delay? Did you have any fears or anxieties or... was it something else which caused the delay?

James: (Long sigh) I didn't think much of the cream they had given me. I didn't think that was working. And that's the only thing they seemed to be doing.

Extract 2

James: [pause 9 secs] That'd be when I went back into errr ... [pause 11 secs] well it was just the doctor came in the room and that's what it..it..he'd had it ex..he took the biopsy, had it examined and it was a cancerous erm item or whatever and... [pause 3 secs] He couldn't..he couldn't deal with it any longer basically. It had to go. And it passed on, I had to go somewhere else. I can't...I can't think of the exact words at all. It was..it was definitely the doctor that came in and told us, told me though.

Extract 3 shows the same difficulty recalling his experiences but ends with a suggestion that James wants to avoid thinking about his treatment: "I'd sooner have it like that then err have it on my mind too long." Indeed, James says, 'I blank my mind to things,' which potentially means that he does so because thinking about some things, such as his diagnosis and treatment for penile cancer, is difficult for him.

Extract 3

James" [pause 6 secs] Err...[pause 7 secs] I went in on the Friday...[pause 10 secs] I think I was operated......I went in on the Friday, I was operated on Friday and I was convalescing over the weekend and I was allowed home on Monday. Erm went in early Friday morning...I think it was Friday afternoon. When I went down. He had a...it was a short notice one when I went in. It was just like a telephone call and...err it was on a bank holiday weekend I went in and...[pause 4 secs] I'd sooner have it like that than err have it on my mind too long.

Interview: Can you remember how you felt leading up to the operation?

James: That I'd like to be going in to get it done. I just felt the sooner the better. Erm a bit erm... [pause 6 secs] a bit better, the trouble is I blank my mind to things.

Uncomfortable Chuckling

James chuckles twice in the interview and the first suggests that what he is talking about makes him feel uncomfortable. In transcribing the PEPC interviews, we added notes in square brackets about information that was difficult to write in words but still potentially added meaning, such as a cough, sneeze, or laughter. The term chuckle was used to denote laughter that sounded suppressed as if it was meant to be laughter and either didn't quite come out fully.

In Extract 4, James chuckles when explaining that sits down to urinate by referring obliquely to what happens when using a urinal ('the pot'). The chuckle is preceded by James qualifying this as 'a little bit awkward' and the suppressed laughter acts as a pause in the conversation that allows us to imagine this situation and perhaps to see it as comedy rather than tragedy. The interviewer's 'erm' shows him thinking about how to phrase the question and sets a tone of awkwardness about James penis and the impact of surgery, which is externalized onto the device for urination ('the toilet'). The interviewer does not return the chuckle, responding with the absence of laughter, what Billig [2005] call's unlaughter, when it could be expected.

Extract 4
Interviewer: So you mentioned earlier that erm the operation surgery has impacted a little bit on erm your ability to use the toilet? How has that changed?

James: Erm... [pause 10 secs] I tend to sit down to err go to the loo, nowadays. It... [pause 4 secs] it tends to come out sideways does the water, rather than straight. Erm which makes it a little bit awkward when you're stood up erm hitting the pot [chuckle]. There's no more I can say really, it's just...I do have a...a funnel, there's a little funnel affair...erm which is very helpful at times erm for directing it.

Emotional Rupture in the Interview

The second chuckle occurs as James introduces the topic of conversation in which he starts to cry and the interview is paused. The interviewer has switched from asking about the physical impact of surgery ('ability to use the toilet' in Extract 4) to the psychological ('self-esteem or confidence'). James responds that there has been no impact and uses the discursive discounter 'but,' orientating the conversation to his difficulties with anger. Rather than asking about the anger, the interviewer asks if James had been offered any support 'dealing with that,' which is followed by a long, loud and uncomfortable sigh. The sigh is the first sign of an uncomfortable emotion and with James revealing that it's occurred since his treatment for bowel cancer we learn that it has been going on for a long time. James sounds open to the possibility of counseling ('Yeah I suppose I could, yeah') although he does start to discount his problem with anger, saying, 'its calmed down a lot' and 'it's not as bad.' As James starts to talk about how 'wonderful' the stoma nurses have been, he struggles to speak and sounds like he is suppressing a cry. As the crying seems to overtake James, he accepts the interviewers offer to take a break.

Extract 5

Interviewer: How about erm your self-esteem or confidence? Has there been any effect on that?

James: [pause 12 secs] Not me self-esteem and not me confidence. [pause 3 secs] But I do get very, very angry, a lot lot quick. I don't know [chuckle] why but I sometimes think it could be that.

Interviewer: Have you been offered any support in terms of erm dealing with that?

James: [sighs, pause 4 secs] No I never asked.

Interviewer: So the hospital didn't offer you any erm emotional or...?

James: No I never asked them, I've never mentioned it before. It's just err[pause 3 secs]... erm...something I do..I do get. I didn't use to get it. It ever seems to have been since the...the bowel cancer operation.

Interviewer: Would you erm consider going on any counselling or anything like that?

James: Yeah I suppose I could do, yeah. I wouldn't...I wouldn't say no, I wouldn't say no...[pause 7 secs] I think it's calmed down a lot though, it was worse after I'd had it done. But it's not as bad as I used to be.

Interviewer: Do you feel as though you have enough support from the hospital?

James: Oh yeah. Anything I want I can get on up there. And the stoma nurses are absolutely wonderful [struggles to finish/starting to cry].

Interviewer: OK?

James: I just get a bit emotional [crying].

Interviewer: Do you want a minute?
James: Mmm? [crying].
Interviewer: Do you want a minute? Just to stop the recording?
James: Yeah you can do if you want, just....[crying].

The interview does resume but James reveals little more about his experiences. Specifically, James says very little in response to the interviewer's questions and answers largely in the negative, such as in Extract 6. The crying is like an emotional rupture that bubbled up and burst through, changing the relationship between the interviewer and interviewee.

Extract 6
Interviewer: How do you now view the future? Has your experience affected your long term plans in any way?
James: No, no, no, no. No it's not affected any plans really.

DISCUSSION

The aim of this chapter was to use a case study to explore areas of healthcare where the deployment of humour or response to patient-initiated humour and/or laughter by a health profession would be considered inappropriate by their peers and/or their patient and/or the patients' family and friends. The case study was selected because the interview contained humour, the researchers felt it would have been inaproprate for them to use humour and the interviewee broke down crying. The case findings show that biographical disclosure was difficult, some chuckling emerged as a release about something uncomfortable and there was an emotional rupture that exceeded the interview, leading to a break.

James difficult, biographical disclosure confirms opinions about no-go areas for humour while expanding them so much that they become pointless. The gradual revelation of a personal story means that we only understand whether humour is appropriate at the end, retrospectively. Consequently, the context is the only information available to health professionals in advance. James revealed that diagnosis and treatment for another condition impaired his sexual functioning, which means that each patient brings with them a personal history that may make humour inappropriate. This means, however, that regardless of the context, humour may be inappropriate for a particular patient. Logically, this extends opinions about 'no-go' areas to all healthcare situations. The problem is that this means that humour is never appropriate, which apart from being refuted by empirical evidence is so broad as to provide no meaningful instruction for healthcare practice.

Branney et al., (2014) show the interaction between men with penile cancer, with discussion moving easily between the participants as they added to, paraphrased and confirmed what each other said and laughed evidenced an atmosphere on *bonhomie*. James difficulty recalling his experiences are a stall to the interaction, with the interviewer's questions and probes for elaboration largely failing. In the second moment of intersubjectivity, the interviewer is finding that their contributions to the interaction are missing their mark, being returned in what could be interpreted as a closed manner, reluctant to talk. The functionalist theory of humour sees interaction as key, particularly for its ability to manage emotions. Difficulties in interaction therefore mean that emotions are poorly managed, which perhaps explains why we, as researchers, felt that humour was inappropriate.

James reports that he cannot urinate without his stream spraying and chuckles when hinting at a situation in which he stands at a urinal and sprays himself and those next to him. 'Laughing about urination' emerged in the workshops with penile cancer patients (Branney et al., 2014) as a release of tension about the difficulties they were facing after treatment. In line with relief theory, James rare chuckle is a release of emotions about something socially unacceptable (urinating on oneself and others).

James tells us that his way of dealing with emotions is to avoid thinking about them and his second chuckle emerges when talking about his difficulties with anger. The chuckle is therefore a way releasing emotions about something socially unacceptable (expressing anger). The success of the humour is brief because James starts to show signs of crying as he talks before being overwhelmed and unable to do more than murmur ('mmm') consent to taking a break. This demonstrates how emotions can break out and exceed a particular interaction. James story of himself is as someone who struggles with emotions and so his talk appears in the interview as something that is laden with emotions, which burst through despite his attempts to suppress them. The functional theory of humour as something that can build through interaction is just as relevant here, with crying. The difficulty with interaction, the long pauses and short answers, gives a feeling, not of *bonhomie*, but of awkwardness. The emotions therefore are poorly managed and erupt, worsening the interaction.

Limitations

A case study lacks variability in the characteristics that might impact on whether humour is appropriate, such as culture, ethnicity and sexuality. Additionally, it is difficult to generalize from a single case. Nevertheless, the point of a case study is to provide insight through detailed analysis. Research could explore a wider range of participants, using theoretical sampling, for example, to identify cases with the potential to challenge our understanding of ostensibly inappropriate humour. Archives of interview-based research about health conditions, such as conducted by healthtalk, would provide ideal resources for secondary analyses to provide such diversity.

This case study is built from a single interview and it would have been useful to have gone back to learn more about, for example, James experience of emotions, particularly anger. A secondary analysis of the interview with James was an excellent opportunity to study a naturally occurring emotional rupture, even if it did occur in the context of a study. Unfortunately, the nature of the PEPC study did prevent follow up with James. While studies might want to leave follow up open as a possibility, the concept of an emotional rupture means that it is to some extent unexpected. A complementary approach is to study cases of an emotional rupture retrospectively, identifying those who have experienced one and exploring what happened.

CONCLUSION

Arguments that humour is ostensibly inappropriate in certain healthcare situations, such as those concerned with sexual functioning, are superficially supported by this case study. A patient's biography is revealed gradually, which means we can only ever decide if humour is appropriate with them retrospectively. This means that the only useful information available to a healthcare professional in advance is the context. Additionally, this case study emphasizes the importance of a patient's biography; if the context suggests humour is appropriate, that patient's personal story may mean that it is not.

A more sophisticated interpretation of this study emphasizes the importance of an integrational-interpersonal approach in which emotions are contained and released through interaction, and the potential for comedy and ridicule lies in incongruities between a patient's experiences and social norms. This case study illustrates an interview when the interaction is difficult. While humour can be used to build rapport, the implication of this study is that it should be avoided when patients are struggling to respond, saying little in response to questions and probes for information and discussion.

Declarations of Interest

The authors have nothing to disclose.

ACKNOWLEDGMENTS

This paper presents independent research commissioned by the National Institute for Health Research (NIHR) under its Research for Patient Benefit (RfPB) Programme (Grant Reference Number PB-PG-0808-17158). The views expressed are those of the author(s) and not necessarily those of the NHS, the NIHR or the Department of Health. We would like to thank Julie Evans (Oxford University) for her guidance throughout the project and the PEPC co-applicants for their support; Kate Bullen (Bournmouth University), Alan White (Leeds Beckett University) and Ian Eardley (Leeds Teaching Hospitals NHS Trust). Last, we are grateful for feedback from the advisory panel members; Brendan Gough (Leeds Beckett University), Kate Hunt (Glasgow University), John McLuskey (Nottingham University), Clare Moynihan (Institute of Cancer Research and the Royal Marsden Hospital Trust), Rebecca Porter (Orchid Cancer), Vijay Sangar (Christie Hospital NHS Foundation Trust & University Hospital of South Manchester NHS Foundation Trust), Sarah Seymour-Smith (Nottingham Trent University), Zoë Skea (Aberdeen University), Anne Storey (Leeds Teaching Hospitals NHS Trust), and David Wilkins (Men's Health Forum).

REFERENCES

Adamle, K. N., & Ludwick, R. (2005). Humor in hospice care: Who, where, and how much? *American Journal of Hospice and Palliative Medicine,* 22(4), 287-290. doi:10.1177/104990910502200410.
Bain, A. (1859). *The emotions and the will.* London: John W. Parker and Son.
Bergson, H. (2008[1900]). *Laughter: an essay on the meaning of the comic (translated by Cloudesely Brereton).* Rockville, MD: Arc Manor.

Billig, M. (2005). *Laughter and ridicule: towards a social critique of humour*. London: Sage.

Branney, P., Raine, G., Witty, K., Braybrook, D., Bullen, K., White, A. K., & Eardley, I. (2013). Clinical practice as research for a rare condition: systematic research review of qualitative research exploring patients' experiences of penile cancer. *Clinical Nursing Studies, 1*(3), 70-76. doi:10.5430/cns.v1n3p70.

Branney, P., Strickland, C., Darby, F., White, L., & Jain, S. (2016). Health psychology research using participative mixed qualitative methods and framework analysis: Exploring men's experiences of diagnosis and treatment for prostate cancer. In J. Brookes & N. King (Eds.), Applied Qualitative Research in Psychology. London: Palgrave.

Branney, P., White, A. K., Jain, S., Hiley, C., & Flowers, P. (2009). Choosing health, choosing treatment: Patient choice after diagnosis of localized prostate cancer. *Urology, 74*(5), 968-971.

Branney, P., Witty, K., Bagnall, A.-M., South, J., & White, A. (2012). 'Straight to the GP; that would be where I would go': An analysis of male frequent attenders' constructions of their decisions to use or not use health-care services in the UK. *Psychology & Health, 27*(7), 865-880. doi:10.1080/08870446.2011.636443.

Branney, P., Witty, K., Braybrook, D., Bullen, K., White, A., & Eardley, I. (2014). Masculinities, humour and care for penile cancer: a qualitative study. *Journal of Advanced Nursing, 70*(9), 2051-2060. doi:10.1111/jan.12363.

Branney, P., Witty, K., Braybrook, D., Bullen, K., White, A., & Eardley, I. (2015). Mortality and sexuality after diagnosis of penile cancer: a participative study. *International Journal of Urological Nursing*, n/a-n/a. doi:10.1111/ijun.12106.

Branney, P., Witty, K., & Eardley, I. (2011). Patients' Experiences of Penile Cancer. *European Urology, 59*(6), 959-961. doi:10.1016/j.eururo.2011.02.009.

Chapple, A., & Ziebland, S. (2002). Prostate cancer: embodied experience and perceptions of masculinity. *Sociology of Health & Illness, 24*(6), 820-841. doi:10.1111/1467-9566.00320.

Du Pré, A. (1998). *Humour and the healing arts: a multimethod analysis of humour use in health care*. Mahwah, NJ: Lawrence Erlbaum Associates.

Francis, L., Monahan, K., & Berger, C. (1999). A Laughing Matter? The Uses of Humor in Medical Interactions. *Motivation and Emotion, 23*(2), 155-174.

Freud, S. (2001[1905]). *Jokes and their relation to the unconscious* (Vol. 8). London: Vintage Classics.

Giora, R. (1991). On the cognitive aspects of the joke. *Journal of Pragmatics, 16*(5), 465-485.

Goffman, E. (1967). *Interaction ritual.* New York: Pantheon.

Gough, B. (2004). Psychoanalysis as a resource for understanding emotional ruptures in the text: The case of defensive masculinities. *British Journal of Social Psychology, 43*, 245-267.

Herxheimer, A., McPherson, A., Miller, R., Shepperd, S., Yaphe, J., & Ziebland, S. (2000). A database of patients experiences (DIPEx): new ways of sharing experiences and information using a multi-media approach. *Lancet, 355*, 1540-1543.

Hunt, A. H. (1993). Humor as a nursing intervention. *Cancer Nursing, 16*(1), 34-39.

Kelly, M. P., & Dickinson, H. (1997). The narrative self in autobiographical accounts of illness. *The Sociological Review, 45*(2), 254-278. doi:10.1111/1467-954x.00064.

Lacan, J. (2006[1946]). Logical time and the assertion of anticipated certainty. In *Écrits: the first complete edition in English: translated by Bruce Fink in collaboration with Héloise Fink and Russell Grigg*, Ch. 9, p. 161-175. London: Norton.

Madill, A., & Gough, B. (2008). Qualitative research and its place in psychological science. *Psychological Methods, 13*(3), 254-271.

McCreaddie, M., & Wiggins, S. (2008). The purpose and function of humour in health, health care and nursing: a narrative review. *Journal of Advanced Nursing, 61*(6), 584-595. doi:10.1111/j.1365-2648.2007.04548.x.

Minhas, S., Kayes, O., Hegarty, P., Kumar, P., Freeman, A., & Ralph, D. (2005). What surgical resection margins are required to achieve oncological control in men with primary penile cancer? *BJU International, 96*, 1040-1043. doi:10.1111/j.1464-410X.2005.05769.x.

Mulkay, M. (1988). *On humour: its nature and its place in modern society.* Cambridge: Polity.

Norrick, N. R. (1993). *Conversational joking: humour in everyday talk.* Bloomington, IN: Indiana University Press.

Oliffe, J., & Thorne, S. (2007). Men, Masculinities, and Prostate Cancer: Australian and Canadian Patient Perspectives of Communication With Male Physicians. *Qualitative Health Research, 17*(2), 149-161. doi:10.1177/1049732306297695.

Pizzocaro, G., Algaba, F., Horenblas, S., Solsona, E., Tana, S., Van Der Poel, H., & Watkin, N. A. (2010). EAU Penile Cancer Guidelines 2009. *European Urology, 57*(6), 1002-1012. doi: 10.1016/j.eururo.2010.01.039.

Shaftsbury, T. E. (1999[1711]). *Characteristics of men, manners, opinions, times*. Cambridge: Cambridge University Press.

Smith, J. A., Braunack-Mayer, A. J., Wittert, G. A., & Warin, M. J. (2008). Qualities men value when communicating with general practitioners: implications for primary care settings. *Medical Journal of Australia, 189*(11/12), 618-621.

Talbot, L. A., & Lunden, D. B. (2000). On the association between humour and burnout. *Humour, 13*(4), 419-428.

Witty, K., Branney, P., Bullen, K., White, A., Evans, J., & Eardley, I. (2014). Engaging men with penile cancer in qualitative research: reflections from an interview-based study. *Nurse Researcher, 21*(3), 13-19. doi:10.7748/nr2014.01.21.3.13.e1218.

Witty, K., Branney, P., Evans, J., Bullen, K., White, A., & Eardley, I. (2013). The impact of surgical treatment for penile cancer – Patients' perspectives. *European Journal of Oncology Nursing, 17*(5), 661-667. doi:10.1016/j.ejon.2013.06.004.

Yin, Y. K. (2009). *Case study research: design and methods*. London: Sage.

In: Humor   ISBN: 978-1-63484-787-2
Editor: Holly Phillips   © 2016 Nova Science Publishers, Inc.

Chapter 7

RELATIONAL PRACTICES OF JOCULAR MOCKERY: HUMOR IN-BETWEEN CONNECTION AND SEPARATION

*Letícia Stallone**

Universidade Federal Fluminense
Niterói, Rio de Janeiro, Brazil

ABSTRACT

Relational work achieved through humorous sequences is in the interest of a number of studies through different perspectives (Holmes & Marra, 2004; 2002a; Stallone & Haugh, forthcoming). However, the investigation of relational work achieved specifically through the practice of jocular mockery has not yet received so much attention (except for Haugh, 2010). The humorous practice of jocular mockery accounts for instances in which the "speaker somehow diminishes something of relevance to self, other, or a third-party who is not co-present, but does so in a non-serious or jocular frame" (Haugh, 2010; 2011). Focusing on the relation between close friends in the city of Rio de Janeiro, from an interactional pragmatics perspective that is informed by research and methods in CA (Sacks, Schegloff & Jefferson, 1974), this paper investigates the relational aspects achieved among these friends through instances of jocular mockery. Building on the interactional achievement model of communication proposed by Arundale (1999; 2010), meanings

---

* leticiastallone@gmail.com.

Letícia Stallone

and interpretings are analysed as "psychological states of individuals that are initiated, confirmed and modified in real time." As a result, jocular mockery is perceived to work either as a means to diminish the possible content of offence of a previous humorous sequence, often downplaying the co-constitution of relational separation in favour of relational connection. Alternatively, it may function as a potential threat, where relational separation outgrows relational connection, especially in contexts in which socially appreciated identity attributes are put into question.

INTRODUCTION

Freud once said that it is always possible to connect a number of people through love, so long as there are others left to receive manifestations of our aggressiveness. When analyzing humor, the fine line between connection and separation produced as a relational result of any interaction is a very interesting and bursting phenomenon.

It is seldom that one finds exclusively bonding and connection provided by instances of humor, most of the times there are misunderstandings, misjudgments and, of course, criticism, antagonism or even aggression between the lines of a joke.

Humor has been receiving a lot of interest in the past few years. As an essentially interdisciplinary phenomenon, it transits among linguistics, sociology, anthropology and many other areas.

Through a linguistic perspective, humor has been taken as a subject for investigation mainly by pragmatics and sociolinguistics, for its social and cultural, as well as its content dependence. More specifically, many have considered the ambiguous aspects of conversational humor (cf. Kotthoff, 1996; Boxer and Cortés-Conde, 1997; Dynel, 2007; Norrick, 1993, 1994, 2003 only to name a few).

In this paper, we analyze instances of a specific kind of humor that has been identified as jocular mockery, mainly by Haugh (2010, 2011). It has been chosen as a subject of analysis because of its frequent occurrence in intimate and close relationships among friends.

Jocular mockery is a specific type of teasing in which the speaker diminishes something of relevance to someone present (be it himself or other) or a third party who is not co-present, but does so in a non-serious or jocular frame. (Haugh, 2010).

We have observed that most of the cases in which jocular mockery occurs among close friends, it reveals itself as a relational practice that – building on identity attributes of participants – can either connect the group as a whole, fostering solidarity and entertainment, or separate the group, forming alliances and promoting disharmony.

We have also observed that jocular mockery is a fundamental tool for interactions among the Brazilian Portuguese speaking close friends analyzed. At times, it seems that producing humor is so important for the group that it is preferred over the need of maintaining harmony in interaction and avoiding conflict.

This paper begins, in the following section, by briefly presenting what has been said about jocular mockery and its occurrence among close friends. We then discuss what it is to treat jocular mockery as a relational practice. In section 3, we introduce our dataset and analytical method, presenting how data was generated and how it is being treated. In the next section, we analyse two excerpts of jocular mockery, the first one displays how it can be seen as a relational practice that fosters connectedness and the second one, in 5.1, how the phenomenon of jocular mockery can disclose separateness. The paper concludes by considering the implications of our study for theorising the role of humour in co-constituting relationships more generally.

2. JOCULAR MOCKERY AMONG CLOSE FRIENDS

Jocular mockery is a very common practice among close friends. At first, the phenomenon may be confused with teasing. The difference between the definitions presented so far of teasing and jocular mockery as specific kinds of humor are very slight. However, it seems deliberate that the categorization of humor takes into consideration the context in which it occurs – both the spatial context and the conversational one.

Keltner et al. define teasing as "an intentional provocation accompanied by playful *off-record* markers that together comment on something of relevance to the target of the tease" (Keltner et al. 2001, 229). This definition ensures two fundamental components of teasing: a provocation and an *off-record* marker that frames the situation as non-serious.

It is the presence of these *off-record* markers that influences the hostile or affiliative effect of the tease. "[P]rovocations with minimal *off-record* markers are likely to be perceived as literal, direct, and aggressive; provocations accompanied by numerous *off-record* markers will be perceived as playful and humorous" (Keltner et al. 2001, 234).

Haugh defines the interactional practice of jocular mockery as a specific form of teasing in which the speaker diminishes something of relevance to someone present (be it himself or other) or a third party who is not co-present, but does so in a non-serious or jocular frame (Haugh, 2010).

Because the term teasing covers such a diverse and heterogeneous range of actions in interaction, jocular mockery restrains itself to a particular subset of teasing where participants are orienting to fostering solidarity, rapport or affiliation.

As a specific kind of teasing, we understand that jocular mockery establishes itself on the two fundamental components of teasing proposed by Keltner et al. (2001), that is, it is a provocation and it brings in its *off-record* marker a degree of hostility or affiliation.

In order to categorize jocular mockery as non-aggressive it is necessary to take into consideration the answers produced by participants and the ways in which the turns are framed by the speaker (Drew, 1987; Pawluk, 1989; Straehle,1993 apud Haugh, 2012).

Thus, Haugh (2012) suggests jocular mockery to be analyzed in three different dimensions: 1) occasioning of jocular mockery in the local sequential context, 2) how jocular mockery is framed by the speaker and 3) how jocular mockery is interpreted by the recipient (the target and/or the audience).

Jocular mockery may be locally occasioned in response to the target "overdoing" or exaggerating a particular action (Drew, 1987), in response to slip-ups or exploitable ambiguity in what the speaker has previously said (or done) and face concerns (Haugh, 2010, 2108).

The "overdoing" in jocular mockery can be related to specific activities such as a complaint or even an exaggerated expression of one's own qualities, such as bragging (Drew, 1987).

In order to convey a jocular frame, speakers use lexical exaggeration, stereotypes, topic shift markers, contrast, contextualization cues, inviting laughter, facial cues and gestures (Attardo et al., 2003; Drew, 1987; Edwards, 2000; Jefferson et al., 1987; Keltner et al., 2001; Lampert and Ervin-Tripp, 2006; Schegloff, 2001; Straehle, 1993 apud Haugh, 2012).

The response to a mockery that is treated as jocular can be laughter (Drew, 1987; Everts, 2003; Glenn, 2003; Jefferson et al., 1987), explicit agreement in acceptance of the jocular mockery and the (partial) repetition of the jocular observation (Drew, 1987; Jefferson et al., 1987).

Laughter on the turn of response, however, does not guarantee that the listener is either agreeing or collaborating with the mockery (Drew, 1987; Glenn, 2003; Haugh, 2012).

Another way of looking at the responses to a potential jocular mockery turn is to observe Hay's strategies of humor support (2001). She suggests that it is possible to contribute with more humor, overlap and offer sympathy; and contradict the previous turn, in terms of self-depreciating humor.

3. RELATIONAL PRACTICES

According to Baxter and Montgomery (1996) interpersonal relationships are characterized by three dialectics – *openness/closedness, certainty/uncertainty* and *connectedness/separateness* – that are not to be identified as individual needs, but as states achieved in interaction by participants in a conversation.

They are called dialectics because, as suggested by the term, they are to be considered as a juxtaposition of conflicting, even seemingly oppositional, ideas and not as one force canceling the other.

We see the antagonistic pairs proposed having to do with different aspects of the interaction; nevertheless, they are impossible to be defined apart from the existence of one another.

Openness/closedness focuses on the individual and its disposition or ability to share. *Certainty/uncertainty* is based on the relationship and how certain participants feel about mutual involvement. It is *connectedness* and *separateness* though that have to do specifically with the relational practices and products of the states achieved in interaction.

According to Arundale (2006), "*connectedness* and *separateness* 'form a functional opposition in that the total autonomy of parties precludes their relational connection, just as total connection between parties precludes their individual autonomy' " (Baxter and Montgomery, 1996 apud Arundale, 2006). That is to say that people in interaction are frequently balancing between being too close or too apart from each other.

The dialectic then presents, on one end, unity, interdependence, solidarity, association, congruence and at the same time, differentiation, independence, autonomy, dissociation and divergence.

When using the dialectic of *connectedness* and *separateness* to re-conceptualize Brown and Levinson's much critiqued distinction between positive and negative *face*, Arundale (2006) seems to agree with the authors themselves when they called for more work from an emic perspective (Brown and Levinson 1987: 48).

The critique on Brown and Levinson, in particular on the notion that negative politeness arises from concern about autonomy of one's actions, claimed that it is an ethnocentric distinction heavily biased towards an Anglo-American conceptualization of politeness.

According to Arundale, the interactional achievement of *connectedness* and *separateness,* different from stating negative politeness as it has been, provides a clear, culture-general conceptualization of negative and positive face (Arundale, 2006: 204).

The dialectic of *connectedness* and *separateness* displays the ever-existing reciprocation between a social system and an individual component in the social system. The interplay between *connectedness* and *separateness* is a dynamic and fluid process in which relationships are not oriented towards canceling out the contradictory poles. "Quite simply, there exists no relationship except as two separate or differentiated persons achieve some form of connection or unity" (Arundale, 2006).

"No relationship can exist by definition unless the parties sacrifice some individual autonomy. However, too much connection paradoxically destroys the relationship because individual's identity become lost" (Baxter and Montgomery, 1996).

4. DATA AND METHOD

Considering the relational dialectics and aiming at an understanding of the practices achieved by interlocutors in close relationships through jocular mockery, we now present the data and method used for the elaboration of the paper.

The data analyzed was taken from a Brazilian Portuguese speaking group of ten close friends who meet at least once a month for long lunches. The meetings take place in the city of Rio de Janeiro, always at the home of one of the participants.

The group of ten participants analyzed was established in 2007. They call themselves *confraria,* a fraternity based on food and friendship. Established as a fraternity, the encounters have as their common goal the meeting of friends who want to spend time together and savor a good meal. The group, consisting of five couples, cook relatively simple recipes that are followed more or less accurately.

The initial idea to title the encounters was conceived when the group had already been meeting frequently for about two years. In these meetings, which were usually held during lunchtime, there were certain regularities, such as the fact of always having a participant cook for the others and thus, certain rules were naturally thought of.

One of the established rules is the prohibition to have a new participant without full consent of all members. The rules that participants refer to were developed in conversations with a lot of humor, however, are complied with stiffness.

As none of the participants is a professional cook, and does not work in the business, there is also the possibility of food preparation go wrong. In this case, the rule is to call a pizzeria and place an order without the complaint of the other participants.

'Everything ends in pizza' seems to be a good image to represent these encounters, although there has not been any situation in which it was necessary to order a pizza, in the recorded data. There are not many discontent assessments in relation to the prepared dishes, but often among the praise, there are suggestions for improvements.

With the consent of all participants, it was then possible to start the generation of data. Initially, the research proposal was received with surprise by the participants. The close relationship between researcher and research subjects proved to be paradoxical. On the one hand, trust guaranteed by intimacy made most of the research subjects feel at ease with the exhibition of their interactional exchanges. On the other hand, also because of trust, questions and concerns about what would be inspected and considered showed up with great concern and fascination.

One difficulty encountered on an early stage of research was the understanding of the scope of linguistics as a social science. There were few participants who could dissociate it from the normative aspects of language study. A widespread concern was with Portuguese mistakes that would be recorded and examined.

It was necessary, then, to clarify the scope of linguistics and interests in the group in question. Initially, what drew attention to these encounters was the number of strategies used that ensured harmony and affection in such a large group and marked by a large age difference. It is noteworthy to say that the youngest participant is 33 and the oldest 65.

Once clarified research interests – at least the initial interests – the participants were getting more comfortable and not only authorized the recording but also collaborated with the invention of fictitious names and help in relation to recording equipment.

The data recording was done in two stages. The first one in 2007 registered 4 meetings, and the second, in 2011, registered 6, one of only 36 minutes. In the first stage, which was recorded for master's research purposes (Stallone, 2009), we used a tape recorder. In the second stage, the recorder was replaced by an mp3 player. Most encounters generated four to five hours of audio. No encounter was recorded from start to finish because of the limited capacity of the recording equipment.

The positioning of the recording equipment varies according to the location of the largest number of participants. There are also silent moments, since often the participants move from the location where the equipment is.

Initially, interest was to investigate interpersonal relationships, especially relationships guided by affection. The focus in humor appears only later on, motivated by its evident recurrence when some excerpts began to be transcribed.

The transcription conventions incorporate symbols of Conversation Analysis (Sacks, Schegloff and Jefferson, 1974; Atkinson and Heritage, 1984) and symbols suggested by Schiffrin (1987), Tannen (1989), Gago (2002) and Haugh (2012).

For data analysis, we identified four sequences containing instances of jocular mockery in the dataset. From these sequences, we selected two excerpts that displayed instances more relevant to the research context.

All the identified sequences containing instances of jocular mockery have humor oriented at *self* – someone else's or the speakers – but in all cases identity attributes are taken as material for humor production.

5. JOCULAR MOCKERY AND *SELF* – TWO SCENARIOS

When jocular mockery is aimed at a participant's *self* it usually involves putting an identity attribute as a target of the humor sequence. We have noted that some identity attributes are held dear by participants and when these ones are taken as a target for humor, there are two possible outcomes.

Our data shows that there is an insistence in the jocular frame, which leads to the conclusion that for the group entertainment and production of humor is very important. However, in the first scenario the target gives in and gives way to the joke, authorizing the jocular frame and eventually going along with it. A friendly atmosphere is then guaranteed.

The second scenario, when the participant does not accept certain identity attributes as a source of humor and consequently does not go along with the joke, shows that the emphasis in a jocular frame can sometimes cause a certain distress to the interaction. Here, there is more threat than pleasure to a joke or a funny remark of any kind and humor gets closer to impoliteness *per se* than to the expected mock impoliteness.

5.1. Jocular Mockery Leading to Connectedness

The extract that follows displays humor being used as a protective tool towards the relationship and thus, generating connection between participants.

The participants are now talking about a movie produced in 2004 by one of the members of the group, Gil. The movie *Olga* is a national production inspired by the life of the communist German, Jew Olga Benário Prestes. The movie becomes a topic in the interaction after Gil gives copies of the DVD to the participants. The extract starts when Gil asks if the friends enjoyed the movie.

EXCERPT 1

1	Dalia	olha eu vou falar porque eu sou sua amiga
1	*Dalia*	*look I will say because I am your friend*
2	Aurora	ih: quando ela vem com ESSAS coisas não é
3		coisa boa↓
2	*Aurora*	*oh: when she comes with THESE things it is*
3		*not a good thing*
4	Gil	fala↓ fala↓ importante ouvir opiniões
4	*Gil*	*say↓ say↓ it's important to hear opinions*
5	Dalia	é?
5	*Dalia*	*is it?*
6	Aurora	fala logo caralho↓
6	*Aurora*	*say soon damn it↓*
7	Dalia	calma: eu não gostei NADA do filme porque eu
8		não acho que a gente tem que se meter pra- a
9		fazer filme de judeu, [de gue:rra a gente
10		não tem nada com isso
7	*Dalia*	*calm down: I didn't like the film AT ALL*
8		*because I don't think that we have to get*

9		*into- do jew films, [of war: we have nothing*
10		*to do with this*
11	Gil	[mas o filme não tá
12		bem feito? eu não fiz- escolhi o ASSUNTO
11	Gil	*[but isn't the film*
12		*well done? I didn't do- choose the SUBJECT*
13	Dalia	AH NÃO isso sim, ta ótimo, a neve tá £super
14		branquinha, [aquela branquela lá tá BEM.
13	Dalia	*OH NO that yes, it's great, the snow is*
14		*£super white, [that white woman is GREAT.*
15	Gil	[AH não sacaneia vai?
15	Gil	*[OH don't tease ok?*
16	Aurora	os judeus- tá quase um £woody allen [((ri))
16	Aurora	*the jews- almost a woody allen [((laughs))*
17	Dalia	[((ri))
18		eu nem dormi.
17	Dalia	*[((laughs))i*
18		*didn't even sleep.*
19	Aurora	teve muitos espectado:res
19	Aurora	*there were lots of spectators:*
20	Gil	((ri)) todos judeus
20	Gil	*((laughs)) all jews*
21	Dalia	((ri alto)) VIU?
21	Dalia	*((laughs loudly)) SEE?*
22	Gil	(2,0) é fazer o que? agora tá feito.
22	Gil	*(2,0) yeah do what? now it's done.*

In line 1, Dalia signals the coming of a dispreffered turn. The first cue is the marker 'look,' which postpones Dalia's evaluation and offers an explanation based on standards of common sense: close friends want the well-being of each other and, therefore, should tell the 'truth.' This way, Dalia prepares Gil for a negative assessment of the film, which is made explicit by Aurora: "ih: quando ela vem com ESSAS coisas não é coisa boa↓" (oh: when she comes with THESE things it's not a good thing – lines 2-3).

Gil seems to dismiss her preface, insisting that the evaluation should be performed (say↓ say↓) and offers a cliché explanation (it's important to hear opinions). Dalia asks for confirmation about the sincerity of the explanation ("is it?" – line 5), signaling that she is aware that professional competence is an identity attribute of great emotional value for Gil. Therefore, she seems to prepare the grounds before issuing an opinion that will certainly displease him.

This preparation is taken with a certain impatience by Aurora, who wants to listen to the opinion and rushes her friend: "fala logo caralho↓" (say soon shit – line 6).

It is then, on the next turn, that Dalia presents her opinion along with the explanation for it: "calma: eu não gostei NADA do filme porque eu não acho que a gente tem que se meter pra- a fazer filme de judeu, [de gue:rra a gente não tem nada com isso" (calm down: I didn't like the film AT ALL because I don't think that we have to get into- do jew films, [of war: we have nothing to do with this – line 7-10).

Gil's answer seems to redirect the matter, shifting the focus to the production of the film, which seems to be an attribute, claimed by him, who, it is noteworthy to say, is the producer of the film, not the writer: "[mas o filme não tá bem feito? eu não fiz-escolhi o ASSUNTO" (but isn't the film well done? I didn't choose the SUBJECT – line 11-12). We see now that Gil wants to limit his involvement in the film as a producer, that is, the care taken by Dalia before announcing her distaste for the film, would apply only if she were to criticize the production of the film and not the choice of theme, as it was the case.

It is now that we observe the use of humor as a means of protecting (or even promoting) the relational connectedness of the interaction. Dalia agrees with Gil: "AH NÃO isso sim, tá ótimo" (OH NO that yes, it's great – line 13) but is ironic with the details of the film production and the performance of the actors: "a neve tá £super branquinha, [aquela branquela lá tá BEM" (the snow is £super white, [that white woman is GREAT. – line 13-14). In a play frame, Dalia reduces the importance of the film production and consequently of Gil's work, to her final evaluation of the film. It is here that we observe a sample of a very common saying in Brazil: "I can lose a friend, but I cannot lose the opportunity to make a joke."

When Gil seems to expect her to make amends, she does not do so and establishes a play frame, which is rejected by Gil: "AH não sacaneia vai" (OH don't tease ok? – line 15). Gil confirms that the frame was a serious one up until now and that was how he wanted it to continue.

However, the play frame is maintained thanks to Aurora on line 16: "os judeus- tá quase um £woody allen [((ri)) (the jews- almost a £woody allen [(((laughs))). She continues threatening Gil's face when comparing his film to the famous Jewish North American filmmaker, Woody Allen. The frame is then confirmed by Dalia, who laughs and jokingly states that the film is not that bad: "eu nem dormi" (i didn't even sleep – line 17-18). And still maintained by Aurora who now talks about the audience as another 'quality' of the film: "teve muitos espectado:res" (there were lots of spectators: – line 19).

Finally, Gil authorizes the attribute to be taken as a joke and joins the play frame, contributing with an input of self-depreciating humor: "((ri)) todos judeus" (((laughs)) all jews – line 20). Now Dalia seems satisfied with Gil's acceptance of the play frame, line 21 and after a long pause, Gil is beaten: "(2,0) é fazer o que? agora tá feito" ((2,0) yeah do what? now it's done. – line 22).

It is interesting to see that even though the identity attribute of a competent professional is a valued one by Gil, he ends up authorizing and joining the play frame, motivated by the shared entertainment that is generated.

We have shown elsewhere (Stallone, 2009; 2015) that humor can take a while to be accepted by the target. However, it seems that when humor has an identity attribute as target and if the attribute is not that much valued – or such as here, if the attribute is shifted into a not so much valued one – it can eventually succeed as a play-frame that generates entertainment and, consequently, connectedness in the group.

5.2. Jocular Mockery Leading to Separateness

Now shifting to the second scenario where identity attributes are held dear and the participant who the humor is aimed at does not give in and consequently does not authorize certain attributes to be made a source of humor.

Most recorded encounters were held at one of the participant's homes, where lunch was being cooked and eaten. This one, however, happens before a lunch that took place in a restaurant but the recording captures the first minutes of meeting at Diego's house.

We have observed that excerpt 2 is a sequence where one of the participants seems to propose a jocular frame, which is accordingly accepted by some participants but not so by the target.

EXCERPT 2

1	Celia	tem que sin- deixa ASSIM↓
1	*Celia*	*have to sin- leave like THIS↓*
2	Jamil	tá bom. olha lá: o:lha?
2	*Jamil*	*it's good. look there: loo:k?*
3	Aurora	[o::lha]
3	*Aurora*	*[loo::k]*
4	Marcela	[UAU:] meu DEUS £que óculos é esse?
4	*Marcela*	*[UAU:] my GOD £what glasses are these?*
5	Celia	[você sa-] ((ri))
5	*Celia*	*[you sa-] ((laughs))*
6	Diego	[£gostou?]
6	*Diego*	*[£liked?]*
7	Jamil	tinha pra homem quando você comprou esse?
7	*Jamil*	*were there for men when you bought these?*
8	Diego	ué como as- não gostou↑ [ca:guei] eu gosto
8	*Diego*	*ué how co- didn't like↑ [crapped] I like*
9	Celia	[((ri))] é lindo
10		<amei>
9	*Celia*	*((laughs)) it's beautiful*
10		*I loved it*
11	Aurora	[((ri))]
11	*Aurora*	*((laughs))*
12	Jamil	po:: hhh lindo?
12	*Jamil*	*damn:: hhh beautiful?*
13	Diego	BOM↓ vamos descer? tô com fome
13	*Diego*	*WELL let's go down? i'm hungry*
14	Celia	foi esse que você trouxe de fora?
14	*Celia*	*were these that you brought from abroad?*
15	Aurora	va- vamos aonde afinal?
15	*Aurora*	*le- let's go where afterall?*

The extract begins with the arrival of the owner of the house, Diego, wearing exaggerated white framed and colorful lenses sunglasses. The sunglasses call the attention of Jamil and Aurora who then shift the topic of the interaction to Diego: "olha lá: o:lha?" (look there: loo:k? – line 2) and "o::lha" (loo:k – line 3).

In line 4, emphasis on the surprise expression "[UAU:] meu DEUS" ([UAU:] my GOD) and Marcela's ambiguous question "£que óculos é esse?" (£what glasses are these?) seem to make Diego think that his choice has gotten approval by the group: "£gostou?" (£liked? – line 6). It is only with Jamil's turn "tinha pra homem onde você comprou esse?" (were there for men when you bought these? – line 7) that Diego realizes the group is making fun of his sunglasses. It is through the contextualization cue of surprise "ué?"(closely translated as 'how come' – line 8) that it is possible to perceive that up until this point in the interaction he probably felt that his sunglasses were being appreciated by the other participants.

Jamil's question redirects the sequence. Diego's homosexuality is a recurrent theme as a trigger for humor in the group, many times initiated by Diego himself. In close relationships among heterosexuals and homosexuals, it seems to be acceptable (and a source of humor) to make fun of the differences in what is considered beautiful and chosen as outfit, but there is a limit as to how far this source of humor can be taken.

Jamil's turn does not find affiliation in Diego, however. Diego disqualifies Jamil's remark when he realizes that his choice of sunglasses was ridiculed: "caguei" (closely translated as 'I don't give a shit' – line 8). In an opposite direction of what the other members of the group do, Diego stands apart from the others stating that what matters is his own opinion: "eu gosto" (i like it – line 8).

Diego's reaction seems to point at another identity attribute seen as non-negotiable as a target for humor. Despite the natural acceptance of a homosexual couple in the group, it is observed that heterosexuals consider "strange" some homosexuals tastes in terms of clothing, accessories, gestures and so on. In a heterosexual only group, Jamil's remark might have not caused discomfort for those who are on the spot. However, here, to Diego, the disapproval of his choices related to his homosexual identity seems somehow to stumble on bad feelings experienced in situations of discrimination.

Diego's surprise seems to be perceived by Celia who makes an effort to repair the unintended threat through a compliment in lines 9 and 10: "[((ri))] é lindo <amei>" (laughs it's beautiful I loved it). Aurora's overlapped laughter, on line 11, can be the answer to the humor intended by Jamil, indicating that to Aurora Jamil's remark may have seemed ordinary and even funny.

Celia's compliment is questioned by Jamil who seems to want to continue the provocation, seeking approval from the rest of the group at Diego's expense: "po:: hhh lindo?"(damn:: beautiful? – line 12). It is then that we can observe in Diego's response that he does not accept Jamil's positioning and rejects the mockery as aggressive and not jocular or playful, making a sudden change of topic with the marker: "BOM↓" (WELL↓ – line 13).

With line 13: "BOM↓ vamos descer? tô com fome" (WELL↓ let's go down? I am hungry), Diego redirects the encounter as a whole and has participants close down their activities and leave the house. Diego's change of orientation shows an abrupt interruption of the previous activity, closing any possibility of a play frame.

There is still an attempt by Celia to make the interaction smoother when she tries to keep Diego's sunglasses as a topic, showing interest with the question: "foi esse que você trouxe de fora?" (were these that you brought from abroad? – line 14). However, the question is ignored by Diego who had already closed the issue back in line 8.

This extract demonstrates that there are certain sacred objects that cannot be taken as a target for humor without jeopardizing the relational harmony of the group. These objects involve identity attributes that are highly valuable to an individual but not as so to the group.

It is observed that it is dangerous to play with someone else's feelings. The maintenance of close relationships, that involve affect and intimacy, require a certain amount of caution in what concerns the pursuit of entertainment. It seems to be important that being funny and generating entertainment does not go over the needs for approval of certain identity aspects perceived as sacred to the other.

Examples such as the extract above are seen as a bad joke, which relates entertainment to impoliteness. On the other hand, we observe that it is through humor that the group organizes itself in order to mend what has been unbalanced and thus making entertainment work so as to maintain the harmony in interaction.

CONCLUSION

In this paper, we aimed at analyzing the relational role of jocular mockery as a specific kind of humor in meetings among close friends. Spontaneous conversations that generate the data investigated reveal that participants perform complex relationships, balancing between the need of a social being and one with its individuality respected.

The meetings are expected to have amenities and light issues as topic for conversations, so jokes and humorous remarks appear as recurring activity.

However, these humorous utterances are ambiguous activities for, on the one hand, they allow for emotional ties and ensure interactional harmony but on the other, the perception of the provocative aspects can cause discomfort and even generate disaffection.

We have observed that identity attributes are frequently taken as a target for humor and even though some topics seem to be avoided, many times generating humor seems more important than considering a 'touchy' topic.

We have also observed that the group takes care of their relationship and does so through humor, making the generated entertainment enhance group bonds. If a jocular mockery is to be uttered and appreciated, it has to be on the grounds of accepted target of humor. If not, the participants will somehow shift the target to that of an acceptable attribute, such as in excerpt 1.

On the other hand, among the avoided topics are those that seem to be sacred, such as in excerpt 2, identity attributes that have a high emotional value to the *self* but not necessarily to the rest of the group.

There seems to be a fine line between a humorous utterance that generates connectedness and one that generates separateness. What seems to count as important data for investigation is the context in which the utterance is produced and, along with it, the relation between what identity attribute is taken as target with the subject who holds the attribute dear (or not).

REFERENCES

Arundale, Robert. 1999. "An alternative model and ideology of communication for an alternative to politeness theory." *Pragmatics* 9 (1):119-153.

Arundale, Robert. 2006. "Face as relational and interactional: a communication framework for research on face, facework, and politeness." *Journal of Politeness Research* 2:193–216.

Arundale, Robert. 2010. "Constituting face in conversation: face, facework and interactional achievement." *Journal of Pragmatics* 42:2078-2105.

Attardo, S., Jodi Eisterhold, Jennifer Hay and Isabella Poggi. 2003. "Multimodal markers of irony and sarcasm." *HUMOR International Journal of humor Research* (16) 2:243-260.

Atkinson, J. Maxwell and John Heritage (Eds.) 1984. *Structures of social action: Studies in conversation analysis.* Cambridge: Cambridge University Press.

Baxter, Leslie and Barbara Montgomery. 1996. *Relating: Dialogues and Dialectics*. New York: The Guilford Press.

Boxer, Diana and Florencia Cortés-Conde. 1997. From bonding to biting: conversational joking and identity display. *Journal of Pragmatics* 27:275–294.

Brown, Penelope and Stephen Levinson. 1987. *Politeness: Some universals in language usage*. Cambridge: Cambridge University Press.

Drew, Paul. 1987. "Po-faced receipts of teases." *Linguistics* 25:219-253.

Dynel, Marta. 2007. "Joking aside: sociopragmatic functions of conversational humour in interpersonal communication." In *Current Trends in Pragmatics*, edited by J. Nijakowska, 246-268. Newcastle: Cambridge Scholars Publishing.

Everts, Elisa. 2003. "Identifying a particular family humor style. A sociolinguistics discourse analysis." *Humor* 16:369-412.

Gago, Paulo. C. 2002. "Questões de transcrição em Análise da Conversa." *Veredas - Revista de Estudos Linguísticos* v. 6, n. 2:89-113.

Glenn, Phillip. 2003. *Laughter in interaction*. Cambridge. Cambridge University Press.

Haugh, Michael. 2010. "Jocular mockery, (dis) affiliation, and face." *Journal of Pragmatics* 42:2106-2119.

Haugh, Michael. 2011. "Epilogue: culture and norms in politeness research." In *Politeness in East Asia*, edited by Dániel Kádar and Sara Mills, 252-264. Cambridge: Cambridge University Press.

Haugh, Michael. "Conversational interaction." In *Cambridge Handbook of Pragmatics*, edited by Keith Allan and Kasia M. Jaszczolt, 251-274. Cambridge: Cambridge University Press.

Hay, Jennifer. 2001. The Pragmatics of Humor Support. *HUMOR: International Journal of Humor Research* 14 (1):55-82.

Holmes, Janet and Meredith Marra. 2002a. "Having a laugh at work: how humour contributes to workplace culture." *Journal of Pragmatics* 34:1683-1710.

Holmes, Janet and Meredith Marra. 2004. Relational practice in the workplace: Women's talk or gendered discourse? *Language in Society*, 33:377-398.

Keltner, Dacher; Lisa Capps, Ann M. Kring, Randall C. Young, and Erin A. Heerey. 2001. Just teasing: a conceptual analysis and empirical review. *Psychological bulletin* v.127 n.2: 229-248.

Kotthoff, Helga. 1996. Impoliteness and conversational joking: on relational politics. *Folia Linguistica* 30:299–325.

Norrick, Neal. 1993. *Conversational Joking. Humour in Everyday Talk.* Bloomington, IN: Indiana University Press.

Norrick, Neal. 1994. Involvement and joking in conversation. *Journal of Pragmatics* 22:409–430.

Norrick, Neal. 2003. Issues in conversational joking. *Journal of Pragmatics* 35:1333–1359.

Sacks, Henry, Emanuel Schegloff and Gail Jefferson. 1974. Simplest systematic for the organization of turn taking for conversation. *Language 50.*

Schiffrin, Deborah. 1987. *Discourse markers.* Cambridge: Cambridge University Press.

Stallone, Letícia R. 2009. "Humor conversacional entre amigos: uma abordagem interacional." Master diss., Pontifícia Universidade Católica do Rio de Janeiro.

Stallone. Letícia R. 2015. "O dilema do porco-espinho: uma abordagem interacional do humor em relações próximas." PhD diss., Universidade Federal Fluminense. Niterói.

Stallone, Letícia R. and Michael Haugh. 2015. "Fantasy humor in Brazilian Portuguese interactions." Paper presented at the IPRA, Antwerp Belgium, July 26-31.

Tannen, Deborah. 1989. *Talking Voices: Repetition, Dialogue and Imagery in Conversational Discourse,* Cambridge England; New York: Cambridge University Press.

BIOGRAPHICAL SKETCH

Name: Leticia Stallone
Affiliation: Universidade Federal Fluminense
Date of Birth: February 19, 1978
Education: graduated in Languages - Portuguese, English and Corresponding Literature from Pontifical Catholic University of Rio de Janeiro (2006). The author has a Masters in Language Studies also from Pontifical Catholic University of Rio de Janeiro (2009), the final paper entitled *Conversational Humor among friends: an interactional approach.* Letícia holds a PhD in Language Studies from Federal Fluminense University in Niterói, Rio de Janeiro (2015), the thesis entitled *The Hedgehog Dilemma: an interactional analysis of humor in close relationships.* She was granted a 3-month scholarship by Brazilian Federal Institution, CAPES, at Griffith

University in Brisbane, Australia under the supervision of Professor Michael Haugh (2014).
Address: Læssøesgade 7, 2, t.v. København 2200, Danmark.

Research and Professional Experience:

2013 – now Studio M'Baraká – Content Writer and Researcher for Academic Purposes (at the moment coordinating the research project entitled *The Hedgehog Dilemma: Humor in Contemporary Arts.*)

2011 – 2012 Faculdade Gama e Souza – Department of Computer Science and Tourism (Business Communication and Academic Discourse Professor)

2010 – 2011 Instituto Isabel – Pedagogy University in Rio de Janeiro (Portuguese and English as a Second Language Professor).

2007 – 2009 Pontifical Catholic University of Rio de Janeiro (Internship with supervisor Clarissa Rollin Pinheiro Bastos' lessons of Portuguese and Academic Discourse).

Professional Appointments:

14th International Pragmatics Conference – Antwerp, Belgium. Fantasy Humor in Brazilian Portuguese Interactions (with Professor Michael Haugh). 2015.

Research Series Seminars – Griffith University, Brisbane, Australia. Fantasy Humor and Jocular Mockery: An Interactional Analysis of Humor in Brazilian Portuguese. 2014.

SAPPIL – Post graduate Seminars – Universidade Federal Fluminense. Fantasy Humor and Jocular Mockery: An Interactional Approach on Conversational Humor. 2014.

SAPPIL – Post graduate Seminars – Universidade Federal Fluminense. The Hedgehog Dilemma: Limits of Play in Close Relationships. 2013.

VII JED – Jornada de Estudos Pontifical Catholic University of Rio de Janeiro. The Limits of Play frame in Affect Relationships. 2013.

IX Congresso Latino-americano de Estudos do Discurso – ALED. Negociação de Identidades em Situações de Humor Conversacional. 2011.

18th Intercâmbio de Pesquisas em Linguística Aplicada – INPLA. Gestão das Relações Afetivas em Situações de Humor Conversacional. 2011.

Simpósio Nacional de Linguagem Humorística. Humor entre amigos. 2010.

VI Congresso Internacional da ABRALIN. Humor Conversacional entre Amigos: Enquadres, Estratégias de Envolvimento e Organização de Preferência. 2009.

XV Congresso da ASSEL. Humor Conversacional entre Amigos: Uma Abordagem Interacional. 2009.

VII Semana de Letras. Humor Conversacional: Estratégias de Envolvimento e Organização de Preferência. 2008.

XXIII Encontro Nacional da ANPOLL – Produção de conhecimento em Letras e Linguística: Identidade Impacto e Visibilidade. 2008.

I Encontro Internacional do GT de Sociolinguística da ANPOLL 2007.

Publications:

Rezende, D (Org.); Stallone, L. R. (Org.) & Seixas, I. (Org.) Virei Viral: Identidades e Coletividades. 1. Ed. Rio de Janeiro: Arte Ensaio, 2014. v. 1. 154p.

Stallone, L. R Como tratar as identidades na pesquisa linguística. Cadernos de Letras da UFF, v. 46, p. 157-171, 2013.

Stallone, L. R. Gestão das relações afetivas através do humor conversacional. via Litterae v. 3, p. 315-332, 2011.

Stallone, L. R & Bastos, C. R. P. A co-construção do humor conversacional para encobrir diferentes objetivos. Calidoscópio (UNISINOS), v. 9, p. 159-168, 2011.

INDEX